SOCCER MIND

Raise Your Game With
Mental Training

Paul M Maher PhD

This edition published in 2023
by DreamEngine Media Ltd

ISBN: 978-1-915212-12-2

Email: publishing@dreamengine.co.uk
Website: DreamEngine.co.uk
Social Media: @DreamEngineuk

Other Books by the Author

Cricket Mind
Bodybuilding Mind
Tennis Mind

CONTENTS

INTRODUCTION

"A lot of football success is in the mind. You must believe you are the best and then make sure that you are."

Bill Shankly

Remember as a child the excitement of wearing your first pair of soccer boots? You then trained yourself in how to use them. You worked on your fitness. You worked on your technical skills.

But what about your mental game? You may be technically gifted, but do you have strategies to turn to when the pressure is on? In Soccer Mind Dr Maher prepares you to reach higher goals, kick away any obstacles, gain control of your thoughts and emotions, and to play every game at your best. See yourself winning, hear the thunderous applause and feel that incredible pride.

Soccer Mind is written for players at all levels, coaches and parents. It is full of practical examples and exercises that you can adapt to make a huge leap forward in your soccer performance and your life.

What is soccer psychology all about? Mental skills training and sports psychology are not modern concepts, they have been around for as long as sports have been played and are as much about mental attitude as solid technique.

The term 'sports psychologist' may intimidate some soccer people. Traditions go back a long way within the established order so new ideas are often frowned upon. Forty years ago acupuncture was laughed at in the West, now it is a fully accepted therapy. The recent titles of 'mental skills coach' or 'performance enhancement coach' are more appropriate and will be better accepted by soccer players as someone who can guide them to use the resources of their mind more effectively and gain a winning attitude.

You have an incredible mind that can sometimes get wired up in a way that is not useful for some situations. Your subconscious mind acts in a literal, even naive way. It is non-judgmental so it will absorb a bad idea as much as a good one. Culture, family, peer pressure or a bad coach may teach ways that sometimes are not useful for what you want to achieve.

Different techniques presented in this manual work for different people in different circumstances and at different times, so be open and willing to experiment. There is more than one way to deal with a particular challenge so take any immediate failure as simple feedback, adapt it, or use another technique.

If you are cynical, think this is all weird, new-age stuff, we need to have a chat. Hundreds of therapists and thousands of sports people say sport psychology does work. There are poor therapists about as there are poor players, so if you or a colleague have tried something like this before and failed, get over it! Sorry to be so blunt. But doom mongers and naysayers will never become better players.

This is very much a 'how to' manual. Techniques are explained step-by-step. It is possible to do them all by yourself, although some may have a greater impact with someone guiding you through the process. Its best for you to refer to them often to develop the necessary competence and refresh your memory, just as you would to develop a technical skill. Being in sport, you should realize the importance of practice, practice, practice. Also consider that by re-reading this book or sections of it frequently you will gain something new and absorbing each time.

Excited? You should be. These methods can rock you to your core. They can also affect other areas of life. Just sit back, put your feet up and enjoy what you learn.

As the word 'soccer' is understood worldwide as opposed to the British term 'football' and since both terms are used identically, I have decided to use 'soccer' throughout for ease of reference.

To win the game, first you must win The Mental Game.

ATTENTION

The information here is intended for people in good health. The ideas, suggestions and techniques here are not a substitute for proper medical advice. Anyone with medical problems of any kind should consult a medical practitioner. The author does not prescribe the techniques covered here as a form of treatment for any physical or mental problems. Any application of the ideas, suggestions or techniques here are at the readers sole discretion.

This publication contains the authors opinion in the subject matter covered herein. The intent of the author is to offer information to help the reader in their efforts to improve their tennis, so makes no warranty of any kind for any particular purpose. If the reader uses any of the information in this publication for themselves or others, neither the author or publisher is liable or responsible to any person or entity for any consequential, incidental or special damage caused or alleged to be caused directly or indirectly for the information contained within.

KICK OFF

"Every single day I wake up and commit myself to becoming a better player!"
Mia Hamm

Most understanding within the soccer community on the mind in sports performance has come from research undertaken in recent years, especially from Europe. Many professional sports clubs there now include a sports psychologist on their medical staff but it is still widely misunderstood in Britain, the attitude here being if you speak to a psychologist there must be something mentally wrong with you.

However as psychology plays an increasing role in shaping a players behavior and performance, many top players today are actively looking for any improvements in helping them perform at their best via their club or individually.

During the 1960s and 1970s while British teams were depending on inspiring speeches from their managers, a lot of research in mental training was being carried out by clubs in Eastern Europe, especially Czechoslovakia and Yugoslavia. Some clubs in Yugoslavia used training simulators almost identical as those used by fighter pilots to speed up their reflexes.

Over the past few decades there has been even more research carried out. AC Milan under Carlo Ancelotti were using psychological support and had a special psychological lab, 'the mind room' for their players.

By playing catch up, the English Premier League introduced the Elite Player Performance Plan (EPPP) in the 2012-13 season for academy players, recognizing the psychological support in development and identity awareness, welfare and education for youths in response to soccer's ever increasing demands.

Clubs already use physical data to record players performance: maximum speed; distance covered; passes completed as well as developments in fitness training and diet. Training a players mental abilities is the next step in developing a player and neuroscience appears to be that next step. The potential is enormous and new products are being researched and becoming available.

In the German Bundesliga psychology has been part of a clubs set up for years. By using expertise in neuroscience and psychology, German company *neuro11* have developed a program that can be integrated into existing set-piece training routines directly on the training ground. By attaching electrodes to the players head, brain states can be measured and an individually-tailored program can be created. In taking a free kick, one player may focus on the ball, another on the opponents wall, others the goal or goalkeeper position. This can be fine-tuned to have the player focused within the right frame of mind.

Other top European sides are trialing brain imaging and virtual reality technology. Some recreate in-game situations taken from thousands of top games that monitor the users responses. This brain scanning technology can also identify neural activity of mood states like anxiety, burnout, depression and insomnia.

As further research is carried out, it seems psychology together with neuroscience will be the future way for soccer to go.

It starts here...

FOR COACHES

*"The measure of who we are is what we do with
what we have."*

Vince Lombardi

Getting the best from players is one of the greatest skills needed by any coach. There is a breadth of variation of players, from difficult to complex, sensitive to laid back. For each player, you must know which individual buttons to push and at the same time, blend them all into a cohesive team unit for it to blossom.

How well you communicate depends entirely on the players response, which means you alone are responsible for how they understand you. Pay attention to the words you use so your thoughts, language and communication becomes crystal clear. There are a number of steps to the methods here, so for the benefit of all soccer coaches, mental skills coaches, team managers, or parents, here are the keys:

Explain the process to your player or players. Establish where they are with a particular mental attitude and where they, or you, want them to be. This is best served by using a scale of 0 – 10, with 0 being no problem at all and 10 being very high. Take anxiety for example. When a young player is about to make a first team debut in a packed stadium, 0 will be no problem, very calm and prepared, while 10 will be extremely anxious with all the variants in between. Having performed one of the techniques, you can then use the scale of 0 – 10 again to test if the young player's anxiety level has reduced.

You need to know is it absolutely right to change the players thinking by ensuring there will only be good, ethical consequences to come from making a change to their mindset. This is best by asking these useful questions:

What is the purpose of this change?

What will the player lose, or gain by it?

What will happen if they make the change?

What will happen if the player does not make the change?

Go on to perform the technique.

Check the technique has worked and your player has improved, remember the scale of 0 – 10.

Future pace. This is asking your player to imagine a future situation which previously would have created their issue and notice how they now feel about it. Repeat this as often as required until your player is convinced their attitude has changed for the best.

Mental skills training is something you do WITH a player, not TO a player.

Pay attention to any non-verbal communication of the player. Is their voice tone, facial expression or body language in accord to their verbal responses?

Although it is rare, but some players may have repressed or traumatic memories which are beyond your ability to change and must be dealt with by a qualified therapist. Some techniques are quite powerful and can have a greater impact than you would realize. Does your player have a history of mental illness or depression? Are they on medication or have a history of epilepsy? If in any doubt, DO NOT work with them.

The biggest factor which prevents a coach involved with children and youth teams from enjoying their role is parents. Some see themselves as second managers and rock the boat because they are emotionally involved in their child's welfare without considering the team. The parents are convinced their child is the best thing to ever happen, so will often challenge the coach regarding team selection and game plan.

Also be aware, parents will often try to impose their own motivations, past regrets and vanished dreams onto their children.

Although time consuming, the coach should meet with parents as near to the start of the season as possible to outline goals and for the children to enjoy their soccer experience.

Some coaches will tell a player when something is wrong but avoid advice on how to correct it. Comments like "you should have done better," puts some players on a long, lonely road. Acknowledge progress and give positive feedback as it motivates, makes players feel good and improves team spirit.

Pep talks pumping the team up, last minute changes, complicated instructions just before kick off can be a distraction to a players mental preparation. Usually these are stress release for the coach. Players, especially at the higher levels know what to do. Yes, players always appreciate encouragement or reassurance on the build up to an important game. After that, most will prefer to be left alone to concentrate during the final minutes before going onto the pitch. Let them know you are available if they need you, then give them freedom to focus on their performance.

Competent coaches will have a great influence on the lives of their players. They are masters of communication and building team spirit. Good coaches care. They support their players, especially if a player is suffering from a loss of form, personal setbacks, or injury. They challenge their players to become the best they can be in a positive and respectful manner which will help them grow. They give players confidence to believe in themselves and making their players feel valued.

A player can be influenced by a clinical sports psychologist or mental skills coach, trained in valuable hypnotic interventions, as these methods can enable change for players who need quick results.

One needs the other...

PLAYER – COACH RELATIONSHIP

*"It's a fine thing to have ability, but the ability
to discover ability in others is the true test."*
Lou Holtz

In soccer there can be many relationships. The player - parent; player - teacher; player - spouse; player - fan. All can have an impact on a players performance. The player - coach role should be recognized as being especially crucial.

A player and coach must develop a relationship based in terms of appreciation, commitment, cooperation, dependence, trust and respect for each other. Overall, the player-coach relationship is a dynamic, but sometimes complex process. Nevertheless, it provided the means by which coaches and players needs are expressed and fulfilled.

Historically coaching has enhanced a players physical, technical and tactical skills. The coach is a major force in promoting the development of a player physically and these days, psychologically, as positive mentoring and support go to create a near perfect working relationship. Positive player growth will develop through empathy, honesty and support.

Soccer coaching implies achievement. The performance of both coach and player is shown as being either successful or not. A coach should be able to listen as well as talk. Good communication promotes the development of knowledge and understanding. A successful and effective coach - player relationship will invariably have positive outcomes for the player in terms of psychological health and well-being along with better performance.

When giving instructions, not only should the coach make those instructions crystal clear, it should be explained to the players why something is being done so they have a clear understanding and feel part of the plan.

In contrast various elements can lead to conflict. Put-downs, critical, sarcastic comments undermine a player's confidence. An ineffective or dysfunctional relationship will be marked by deceit, lack of interest, lack of commitment, remoteness, even antagonism and abuse. Ethical and professional issues that are associated with codes of conduct to protect players and coaches run a risk of being breached. Misunderstandings may develop if the coach fails to accurately understand the players intentions or emotions.

A perfect working relationship involves an ability or even desire to understand the other persons meaning and feelings with a strong, improving mutual liking, trust and respect.

The task of a coach in developing an effective relationship that players can use for growth and development is a challenging one because it is a measure of the growth they have achieved in themselves. This implies a responsibility on the part of coaches in that they must continually strive to develop their own potential, as this will be reflected in the maturity and growth of the player.

Let's look at the lifespan of a soccer player...

A PLAYERS EVOLUTION

*"You have to expect things of yourself before
you can do them."*
Michael Jordan

Throughout a soccer players career, there will be many transitions, ranging from playing at school in their first pair of boots, to eventually retiring from the game and perhaps going into coaching. Players at all levels may take these transitions in their stride or have a hard time accepting them. Techniques in this manual may help overcome these transitions.

So, lets consider the evolution of a soccer professional Tom, of course, this does not represent an exact evolution and depends on the structure of the country, league or club.

Child. Before the age of eight Tom has a limited concept of the world around him, thinking he is the center of that world so making it difficult at an earlier age to integrate into a team sport. It is best for Tom to gain experience at the skills of soccer and game results should not matter so much.

Tom will begin playing at school from personal interest or because an influential adult has given encouragement and may be scouted and signed by a club in the eight or nine age group. Only the best advance to the older age groups, the rest released at the end of each season.

As Tom grows older, he feels a strong need to have his worth confirmed or appreciated. If his parents and coaches show encouragement, are not too demanding of Tom's performance, it will become a positive development in Tom's self-esteem while too much pressure from insecure parents can harm his development.

Junior. There can be conflict with adult authority as Tom wants to make his own decisions regarding technique or tactics and may find it difficult to accept the position chosen for him on the playing field. Finding a role model or mentor may ease troubles. It is rewarding to be accepted and liked by team mates.

Youth. Reactions are much more emotional. As a teenager Tom is a confused mess, searching for self identity while remembering childhood experiences and looking toward the future without any reassurance by the present. Also there is a contradiction going on in his mind from disagreements with adults and a desire to be like them.

Academy youths have to deal with many demands, pressure comes from competition for team places, training maybe four times a week while being constantly judged by coaches at the same time studying for exams.

When important games come around, some may think more on the difficulty of the game and the opposition than their own physical ability. Avoidance can be an antidote with complaints of feeling ill and any small injury can be an excuse not to participate. Promising players may even give up soccer completely to escape their perceived pressures.

Professional. Only 10% of academy players will sign a contract to become a professional player. Our Tom will begin to make sacrifices to become more competitive, he will not accept any limitations on technique and will work exceedingly hard to master any weakness in order to improve. Hard training and frequent selection disappointments can make Tom consider his role at the club or in the soccer world.

For the new professional, perhaps living far from home could create a certain amount of stress. New relationships may become negative experiences, caused by new acquaintances who will try to benefit from the players position rather than out of true friendship. Often the local press is ready to report on any behavior as the player begins to cultivate their own image. Scandal, no matter how exaggerated, sells newspapers.

Tom breaks into the first team, usually by making appearances as a substitute. Players in this situation are frequently under pressure from coaches, supporters, the media and team mates which, in some cases, can go to increase the players fear of failure.

Tom becomes established in the first team, or left on the bench for extended periods through rotation. Now he is prepared to take risks and be impulsive. This may also create a lack of motivation and lapses in concentration, so it is important for Tom to continue to work hard at the physical demands of competitive soccer, with personalized psychological methods that will overcome any negative factors and enhance his sporting performance.

International. Being chosen to represent country at Under 21 level. Becoming more sure of life's direction and he will begin to make plans how to accomplish further goals in life. Sometime in the near future if not already, commitments regarding marriage and family come along.

Winning a major trophy. It is possible for a player from the lower leagues to reach promotion to a higher level at a particular point in their career. Older players concede when they won a major trophy at a young age they did not appreciate it as much as when they became more experienced or emotionally what they have achieved.

Tom now becoming a full international and seasoned pro, even club captain. He's old enough to know what he should do to keep playing at the highest level possible. He's always in the squad when fit and wants to play every game.

Becoming a senior player and already a role model or mentor for juniors. By now running the first five yards in his head. Risk-taking declines with a cautious fear of failure. As Tom realizes he is getting older, maybe no longer the club's star player, maybe no longer chosen for international duties, this can upset his frame of mind. Perhaps changes at boardroom level or coaches may demotivate him. However, players over thirty who still maintain their fitness and enthusiasm can give a great deal to their team from their knowledge and experience.

Slowing down and making cameo appearances, his playing is rationed now and spending longer on the bench. A transfer to a lower club is likely. For a player who has experienced success, there is a danger that they can no longer find stimulation or motivation. Self-image has changed and aware of that. A phenomenon known as *'the hypnosis of social conditioning'* comes into play. What this means is the player is already programmed to expect his body to begin to break down and wear out. Consequently, as Tom gets older, the expectation becomes reality. The good news is there is nothing in medical science saying his body will fall apart after the age of thirty five!

Retirement. Tom misses more games than he plays. He may start to take another look at his career, home, even his partner and may become more self-interested. Once a soccer career has gone it creates a void in life with a feeling of helplessness and doubt. Self-image and confidence suffer and he is searching for a safety net when he is no longer playing. The big question on Tom's mind is "what am I going to do?"

Retiring players still have a lot to offer. They can contribute knowledge to younger players and become involved with the youth set up if the club has one to effectively become a role model and mentor to juniors. Passion can itself create new opportunities, perhaps leading to coaching, leadership positions, teaching, writing, counseling or public speaking.

Attending various coaching courses to stay in the game as his playing career is almost over. Tom may take a coaching position with a smaller club and if successful and wise, begin to work his way up to higher leagues. As he heads into his fifties, he could start to settle down from renewed energy and a fresh zest for life.

But watch State Control...

STATE CONTROL

"At a football club, there is a Holy Trinity. The players, the manager and the supporters. Directors don't come into it. They are only there to sign the cheques."

Bill Shankly

Emotions run high in soccer. It has become a results business. It's trendy for corporations to invest in a club using their vast millions for a top side, or down to a local butcher or engineering firm sponsoring the kit for a youth team. A new chairman can be the best thing that has ever happened to the club, or the worst.

Once a club reaches company status, it wants to sell merchandise, television rights, wants to be seen as forward thinking — a stylish, modern corporate body seeking a solid media image. This brings expectations from chairmen, the board of directors and shareholders. A club which is in business does not function through sentiment.

Supporters want their team to accomplish something through a hard fought season. They are desperate to see their heroes win honors. They also have their expectations and follow a ritual every weekend which for some fans becomes a religious experience.

Coaches, referees, club and association officials, sponsors and agents all have an involvement. But it is the players who invest their time and energy to accomplish success, either at club level or personal success.

With so much being at stake for so many people around the globe, this need for success leads to strong emotions and various psychological implications for everyone involved. Seen by sobbing uncontrollably after a missed penalty, throwing tea cups across the changing room, sheer elation from winning the World Cup or near suicide for losing it.

Many players find themselves when they are in 'a right state' before or during a game, instead of being in 'the right state' and so unable to perform effectively or worse, embarrass themselves and their club. A bad referee decision can make some players see red. We will take a look at problems such as anger and how to deal with them later on.

For the majority of experienced players in the top leagues, they are likely to assume any nervousness as Adrenalin and motivation to perform well, more so than players in the lower leagues. Having said that, let's not forget the many giant killers in the FA Cup who were able to beat much superior opposition because they reached a level of performance intensity far higher than the 'big team' could.

The mood enhancement techniques you will learn here will teach you valuable tools and approaches to use so you will be able to manage confidence and energy levels, or help the players you deal with, especially before and during an important game.

Let's look at the workings of the mind...

YOUR MIND

Every stadium, every new formation, every team selection ever made began with just one thought. You should appreciate what you focus on, you get more of so the thoughts and words you use need to be formed to produce positive direction.

What you focus on is what you get so if you think you are tired, you will become so. Imagine how that thought can affect you in a cup final when the ninety minutes are nearly up and you are facing extra time!

Conditions have a bearing on you such as weather, ground state, stadium atmosphere or the importance of the game. When you simplify everything down to its basics, there is no difference between defending a corner in the first minute of a game, or defending a corner in the last minute. The difference is your response to the situation. It's not what happens that is so important, but rather, how you perceive it which is down to your mental attitude.

By understanding how your mind works you will be able to utilize its power and get the most for yourself or those you coach. It's often said we use less than ten percent of our mind. Most of its enormous latent power is still unknown to medical research.

Your mind has two parts, the conscious mind and the subconscious mind also known as the inner mind, or unconscious mind which is a mistake as it's not unconscious. Some spiritual believers also claim we have a super-conscious mind.

What we do understand is the conscious mind consists of approximately 10% of your whole mind. It functions in a state of active awareness. You are aware of reading this book right now. You are aware of the words on the page. Your conscious mind thinks and plans. You consciously set goals and targets, plan tactics, decide what skills to learn or practice in training. You consciously decide how you are going to take a free kick and where you are going to place it.

Your subconscious mind has much more depth to it. It contains all your memories, your beliefs and values and runs your bodies functions. Are you aware of your breathing? Of your digestion? Who regulates your temperature? And most importantly, who controls your emotions? Your subconscious! Using the above free kick example, having decided consciously where you are going to place the free kick, your subconscious takes over by coordinating all your physical movements which have developed from constant practice.

The goalkeeper, defending your free kick, will be unable to react consciously as he has no idea where you are going to place the ball and as the ball could be traveling at well over 80 mph will have to react instinctively.

This is why you practice. The subconscious mind will find it difficult to perform a task it has never seen or executed. The better you practice, with constant repetition, the more automatic, competent and smooth your reactions become. When it is not possible to physically practice, you can use your imagination.

With imagination your subconscious responds to symbolic thought. It sees, hears, feels, tastes and smells. Imagine taking that free kick. See the ball in your mind's eye. Hear the sound as you kick the ball and the fans chant your name. Imagine you can feel your foot connecting and smell the freshly cut grass as you guide the ball toward the top corner of the net.

The conscious and subconscious minds can best be described using this analogy. The conscious mind is the team manager, planning tactics, setting targets, analyzing the opposition. It's the task of the team – the subconscious mind, to follow the manager's instruction and make his plans happen on the field.

While there is good communication between the manager (conscious mind) and the team (subconscious) and the team is well drilled in its duties, they should play efficiently. If there is poor communication brought about by low confidence, negative thoughts, poor skills, misunderstandings, then you can imagine what the performance on the field will be like with the manager bellowing uncontrollably from the technical area.

Staying with our free kick example, when you have chosen consciously where to place the ball then you change your mind as you are about to shoot, you interfere with your bodies natural flow, creating poor communication between manager and team, poor communication between conscious and subconscious.

That is why practice is so important, especially when working on new tactics or improving specific skills. The more you practice, the more automatic movements become for you, so you are better able to reproduce them without stopping to think during a game. Remember this - perfect practice makes perfect performance.

Your subconscious is like a loyal servant. It wants to serve you. However, it need guidance. It responds best through your senses rather than words. Therefore, sights, sounds, feelings, smells and tastes are much more helpful in making your subconscious mind learn what you want it to do.

Let's talk about you...

WHAT ABOUT YOU?

"Be yourself, everyone else is already taken."
Oscar Wilde

Your behavior is a result of your self-image, the person you believe you really are. Your self-image is so strong, your behavior will have you perform consistently as the person you think you are.

We all know people who are skilled, yet think they are not. They think they are too fat, too slow, too old, whatever. If you believe that about yourself, if you believe yourself not good enough in any way, you will unconsciously sabotage any effort to make yourself a winner.

Studies have proven time after time, an extraordinary number of sportspeople fail because they think themselves less than they are worth through this limited self-belief. Are they unworthy? Of course not. It's how they see themselves in their imagination which affects their performance and may even cause self-destructive behaviors.

Here is an example to prove my point. Sit for a moment somewhere quiet and remember some time in the past when you felt tired, sad, despondent. Really get back into that time by remembering everything you could see and hear in as much detail as you can. Bring back any physical or emotional experiences, get that memory and keep it in mind for a few seconds, then try to stand up.

Now, sit down again and this time, bring back to mind a time when you felt energetic, determined, optimistic. Again, remember in as much vivid detail as you can what you saw, hear the good things that you heard and get in touch with the physical or emotional feelings you had and keep them in mind for several seconds. Now stand up.

Compare the two experiences. In the first you may have found it an effort to stand. How about the second? Did you leap up ready to go? Isn't it interesting that in just a few seconds, thinking one way then another, created an entirely different result. Your thoughts influence how you perform. Your belief about yourself influences your thoughts, which affect your behavior, as this book will prove. I'll discuss the importance of belief more in the next chapter.

That said, let me remind you how quickly a soccer career goes by. For instance, it's incredible how the last twelve months have gone by. How was it for you? Think about your mortality. Imagine your breathing your last. Did you achieve all you wanted to do in soccer? Did you truly live it? Play at the grounds you always wanted? Enjoy wonderful moments with your team mates? Before you know it, you find yourself retired, then into old age and there you are, reflecting on how good you could have been. This is how it ends up for the vast majority of players. Where did all the time go?

The only thing you have total control of in this world is your thinking. At first you may feel self-conscious trying out these methods. Whenever you do something new that takes you beyond your comfort zone you feel apprehensive. It's OK, your human! You must grit your teeth and get out of your comfort zone and challenge yourself.

This book will open up to you clear ideas as to what you need to do to create the future you want. Nothing in your life is going to change unless you change. You are fully capable of mental and physical feats. You are bigger than you think, capable of more than you can imagine.

You are now in the process of thinking with belief...

BELIEF

"Man is what he believes."
Anton Chekhov

You are about to take a penalty. You need focus, courage and self-control to outwit an aggressive keeper trying to psych you out. Belief gives you the assurance to trust in your ability.

Belief dominates behavior whether positively or negatively and behavior affects performance. Your physical behavior is controlled by belief. A belief is knowing with absolute certainty what something means to you. That belief can mean the difference between an ordinary player and a cup winner. Success or failure – you always prove yourself right. A lower league player can improve and rise in leagues with the desire belief can bring.

Whether you believe you can do something or believe you can't, you are right!

Belief in your ability determines the level of success you will achieve. Once you realize the benefits changing limiting beliefs can do for you, you will have much more motivation to change those limiting beliefs and become a more accomplished player. Performing at or even near, your true potential can be as rewarding in itself for some as a winners medal can be for others and one of the reasons why people are happy playing soccer.

In other ways belief can determine your quality of happiness, health, wealth and success. What you believe even has a greater influence on your life than the actual truth.

Notice the successful players. They made more mistakes than those who have not. Every mistake has been accepted as a learning opportunity by them. They continued to believe in themselves. Failure is part of the learning process, not the end of it. It's only a frustration.

Whether you believe you can do something or believe you can't, you are right!

When have you failed? Only when you stopped believing. Every response is information to tell you what actions are getting you closer to, or further away from what you want.

We all get stuck in our beliefs, however sensible we think they are. You may find this interesting. You tend to believe what you think is true without question. If you believe you don't have a good first touch, it's because you believe you don't have a good first touch and you will forget any memory of when you performed a good first touch. But the interesting thing is, if you tell yourself you do have, that then gives you permission to question that defeatist belief and soon, with consistent practice, you will find that you develop a good first touch. You will begin to adopt the proper physiology to receive the ball. What you first believed was not necessarily real, you just needed to invest in yourself. Confused? The nice thing about being confused is you come out of it with something new.

Belief creates self-talk, how you speak to yourself inside your head. I'll discuss that later on. In the meantime, if you are going to say something to yourself, you may as well make it something good.

Whether you believe you can do something or believe you can't, you are right!

Take a belief which is holding you back.

Think about or write down it's opposite, more positive belief.

Imagine what it would be like living the more positive belief.

Believe that:

You do have the ability to succeed.

You can accomplish anything.

There are no problems, just opportunities.

You are creating your future now.

If you believe you are destined to become a successful player, you will be.

Now that kind of belief can give you a buzz you won't believe!

And the penalty? Assert your authority. Be confident in the face of the goalkeepers hostility and believe the ball is there to be booted into the net!

Whether you believe you can do something or believe you can't, you are right! - Am I getting the message across?

Next, believe in the power of imagination...

IMAGINATION

*"The success I have at free kicks is five percent skill
and ninety five percent successful imagery."*
Giofranco Zola

Imagine that I have just cut a lemon in two and I've handed you one of the halves. Notice it's texture in your hand as you bring it up to your mouth. Be aware of the citric smell while you place the juicy fruit in your mouth. Now, suck on all that tangy lemon juice and let it run down your throat.

As you are reading this, imagine you have submerged both of your hands in a bucket of hot, soapy water. You can imagine what that feels like? Did you have a bath last night, wash the windows, even your car? Recall that feeling of hot soapy water on your hands, make it vivid, feel those pinpricks of watery heat.

Your subconscious mind cannot tell the difference between a real or imagined event. It's just like a DVD recorder! It records sights and sounds continuously. Your body then treats every vivid thought and image as if it was real.

Notice how your body responds to the vivid use of your imagination more so than a conscious command. If you order your heart to speed up, it will not. If you imagine in detail, walking down a sinister, dark alley late at night and hear fast, approaching footsteps coming behind you, I bet your heartbeat will increase. Ever awakened from a nightmare? It wasn't real but you woke up in a sweat, your heart pounding, gripped with fear and it took a while for you to calm down.

Some people claim they cannot visualize, as they don't see in pictures clearly. That's OK, just have a sense of a picture in your mind. It does not have to be as clear as your vision while reading these words. Everyone has the ability to imagine, I may have just proven it to you. If not, answer these questions:

Think of your locker in your changing room. What does it look like? Where is the door handle? What sound does it make when you shut it? To answer, you have to use your imagination.

Now, by changing the pictures and sounds of your mind, you can gain conscious control of any aspect of your game. Images that are bigger, brighter, bolder have a greater impact than those which are smaller, duller and further away. Let me show you.

Think of someone you found stressful to play against or who rankled you. Think about facing them again. Notice how the bad memory of that person can hurt you like a knife. They can beat you without a ball being kicked. Here is something you are going to love. Recall their face. As you do, ask yourself:

Is the memory in black and white or in color?

Is their face in your memory to the left, to the right, or there right in front of you?

Is their face large or small?

Is the memory light or dark? Moving or still?

Are there any sounds?

Now, play around with the way you remember that person. Make each of the following changes in turn and notice what happens:

If the memory has color, drain it all away until it is like a black and white photo.

Move the position of their face and push it further away from you. Shrink it down in size.

Turn down the brightness, make it fuzzy.

If the memory is moving, freeze frame it. If still, animate it.

What sound do you hear? Is it their voice? Change it by giving them a squeaky voice like a cartoon character, or a deep, sexy one, go on, do it.

Finally, give the face a clown's nose, or bright colored hair, Mickey Mouse ears. Go on, have fun!

Altering your memory can change how you feel. Think of that person again in this new way. How do you feel about them now? Probably the stressful memory has diminished if not gone completely. Not only do you feel different about it now, imagine how much more comfortable you will feel the next time you face that person. It's your control, your emotion, your thinking that belongs to you, not someone else controlling you.

***

Mental training through imagination is an essential tool in the soccer player's arsenal. Professional sports people understand the importance of rehearsing skills often in their minds. They become so well prepared, they are able to go into autopilot when they need to use those skills for real. Most soccer activities are done subconsciously. Do you deliberately think about the physical actions of taking a throw in? Taking a free kick? Jumping to head the ball? Of course not, you do them naturally.

Here is how you can imagine playing a whole game. If you visualize the whole game minute by minute in normal time, it would become very tiresome. You know the key events that affect your position throughout the game so speed up the game in general at super-fast speed, but when you come to the parts which involve you, bring it back to normal speed.

Imagining different scenarios helps prepare you for any eventuality during a game. One key to successful imagination is dealing with unforeseen challenges and problems that happen before, during and after a game. Make a list of things that could go wrong and then practice overcoming them and you will be better prepared for all possibilities. Regardless of what problem you face during the game, imagine it turning out right for you.

***

Let me show you how to use imagination in a way known as *association and dissociation*. This is where imagination skills really pay off. *Association* means re-living the event as if it is really happening, seeing through your own eyes, hearing the sounds through your ears and feeling all the feelings. *Dissociation* is noticing the situation as if you are watching yourself as in a movie. As you are more detached from the action, there is less emotional impact.

Think of a stressful or uncomfortable memory, maybe an own goal. How did you feel? Keep that image in your mind. Now step out of yourself so you can see the back of your head. I know you may be skeptical, at least give me a hearing. Now move as far away from that situation you are remembering as you can. Step all the way out of the picture, so you can still see it, but way over there somewhere, as if it is happening to someone else. Shrink it down. Drain all the color. Turn the background fuzzy or white. Fade away any sound. Notice by dissociating reduces the intensity of the feelings you were having. Do those emotions feel less now? It takes courage to learn new skills such as these.

You can do the same to heighten a good memory with association. When you think about happy memories you re-create the happy feelings associated with them.

Remember a game when you felt really confident, aware of your ability, strength and self-belief. Now let that image come into your mind. Make it juicy. Step into that memory as if you were there again, seeing through your own eyes, hearing through your own ears and feeling how successful you felt throughout your whole body. Enlarge the memory, make it bigger and brighter, the feelings stronger, turn up the sounds, make everything richer. If you cannot remember a time, imagine how it would feel to be totally confident – you get what you focus on.

There you have it. To reduce a negative memory, step out, move away from it *(dissociate)*. Watch it as if it is happening to someone else. Shrink it, turn it black & white, dull, out of focus. Make the sounds quieter, further away. Doing this can cause any bad emotional response to drain away. Notice how you are controlling how it affects you.

And to improve a positive memory, zoom in and fully experience it *(associate)*. Make the image bigger and closer, intensify the color, increase the brightness, make the sounds closer and louder unless it is a memory of peace and quiet. Live it. You can have a great deal of fun playing with these methods.

***

Here is an experiment. Players in other positions can adapt this for themselves. You are a striker and for some reason you have lost your greed and the goals have dried up. Psychologically it is becoming an issue as you keep re-running those missed scoring chances in your head.

First imagine yourself sat on the sub's bench (associated) during a past game, watching yourself on the field (dissociated). What encouragement and advice would you give that you who is playing? Let that mental film run while you watch yourself and stop the film at a point just before 'he' missed a goal scoring chance. Being dissociated, this should help you remember the moment but without the negative emotional content.

Freeze frame that image. Here is where you get to have fun. Play with the image. If it's in color, drain the color away and turn it into black & white, If it's vivid, de-focus it. Change any sounds and their location. Change any feelings.

Rewind. Start the movie again in all it's glory. Make everything real and speed it all up until you reach the point just before 'he' failed to score.

Now associate, leaving the bench and instantly becoming yourself on the pitch. Go through everything at normal speed and adjust anything needed so it turns the missed scoring chance into a goal. Notice as you send the ball into the net.

After celebrating the goal with your team mates and feeling how good you can feel, dissociate from the pitch and go back to the bench. Applaud your goal scorer, give useful feedback and repeat that visualization several times until it begins to feel like a real memory.

***

Imagine you are defending. Step into a movie of yourself controlling the ball, tackling, volleying, clearing and heading almost at will. Feel mighty and proud. Hear the thud of every perfectly struck ball. Notice the opponents – forwards, midfielders. Shrink them down and turn them into black & white, move them further away from you, duller, quieter. None of them able to make any penetration. Now do the same yourself, this time as a winger – go on, I'm not going to do everything for you!

***

You can use your imagination to free yourself from any old, negative beliefs that might be limiting you. That's right! Imagine they are written or painted on a wall. With a ball at your feet, boot it at the wall so you demolish the wall completely. See the dust, hear the bricks tumble down, feel the energy you are using until those negative words or images are totally destroyed.

You could imagine them drawn or written on paper. Feel the paper between your hands as you rip it to shreds, hear it, feel it, see it happen there in your mind's eye. Finish off by ritually burning it. I said some methods would challenge you – this is all revolutionary stuff.

Here is an easier one. Close your eyes and imagine in your mind a picture of the player you wish to become. See yourself in your kit, your balanced stance, the confident expression on your face, all the tiny details. Take that picture and throw it up into the air and multiply it so that hundreds of copies come raining down all around you as far as you can see. They even go into your past and future.

Did that feel awkward? Exercises like these may seem silly at first, but while you control the pictures in your mind and how they sound, you are not at the mercy of anyone else or circumstances and they direct your subconscious mind toward being the soccer player you want to be. A flame will ignite inside you.

Maybe imagine once or twice not doing as well, so you can bring all your emotions into it. Do not just imagine the best-case scenarios. Be prepared with a plan B and a plan C. Do not imagine failing, but mentally plan how you will respond to unpleasant or difficult situations. This happens sooner or later when games do not go exactly as hoped. You can still be proud of putting 100% effort in.

I'll teach you next about self-talk...

SELF-TALK

Also known as internal dialogue, self-talk is simply the way you talk to yourself inside your head. You worry over a bad pass, congratulate yourself after a good result, even tell yourself how sexy you look in your fresh, clean kit. People do it every day, but mostly it's negative. Blaming yourself, chastising yourself, saying "I'm not good enough; I'm too tired; I'm too old." This is one of the major causes of poor performance. If you tell yourself something often enough, you will begin to believe it. It may not be true, but you will certainly believe it is. If you have negative beliefs, you have negative self-talk, which will confirm the negative belief, and so it goes on.

While positive thinking may not always work, negative thinking almost always does. Be aware of your internal dialogue. If the voice you use is not supporting you, change it!

A major problem for sports people is dwelling over poor performance. This memory leads to negative self-talk along with emotional discomfort. A pessimistic mind may then remember similar bad events. Allowing the past to affect you instead of focusing on the present only slows you down. You suffer tight muscles, energy loss, poor coordination, which add to the bad memory.

Be good to yourself when you talk to yourself by talking positively. Make mental pictures of yourself being a total success. See yourself winning. Hear the congratulations from your team mates, the applause of the spectators and feel how good you feel when you practice being a winner. Mental rehearsal is the next best thing to actually being successful, so do it as often as you can and review it with positive self-talk. You will be delighted when you witness your future.

What do you say to yourself when things go wrong?

What do you say to yourself when confronted by a challenge?

Confident players will talk differently to themselves than those who lack confidence, even though they perform equally well. Playing with confidence gives you the security to enjoy every minute and will be reflected in your game. Without that confidence, another player may always feel unprepared, nervous, undecided. Those thoughts will then reinforce those beliefs. So you see how vital confident, positive self-talk is.

Keep track of those positive or negative thoughts you have about yourself so you can change any negative thinking to a more positive outlook. Making positive affirmations will help you feel more confident. But to work effectively, these affirmations need to be inspiring and practical. Boastful declarations such as "I'm the best player in the league" or "nobody can tackle like me" become banana skins and you will end up looking foolish, so take care.

Affirmations such as "I am prepared and ready to defend" repeated slowly and thoughtfully can lead to calmness. This gives you a positive mindset and leads to clear thinking and good judgment.

Are you holding yourself back through perfectionism...

PERFECTIONISM

*"I don't care what you say about me,
just spell my name right!"*

P.T. Barnum

Perfectionism does create positive qualities. An ambitious drive to succeed, to plan and organize and a focus on developing excellence. These people can be highly effective and energetic.

A perfectionist can get hung up doing things perfectly. Perfectionists can be their own worst enemies because they are never satisfied with their performance. A self-critical perfectionist can never be perfect because of fear of making mistakes. That is the greatest barrier to success. Beneath the desire to succeed and reach excellence, a perfectionist often has an ultra-negative, condemning voice going on inside their head.

A perfectionist hates to lose, but a perfectionist must not get anxious about losing.

For some perfectionists, anything less than 100% is unacceptable. Even when playing well, they are unable to feel any real fulfillment, as in their eyes, they never do anything of sufficient high standard to warrant feelings of satisfaction.

Perfectionists easily become discouraged by failing to meet the impossible aspirations they set for themselves. Inefficiency, inconsistency, delays and poor results can create a reluctance to take on new challenges so they accomplish less rather than adjust their ambitions more realistically.

Striving to be too perfect can create failure. Fear of losing, making mistakes, the need for control, obsessions or unrealistic expectations all cause anxiety, misery, dissatisfaction. Team mates and family can be offended as the perfectionist can be as critical of others as they are of themselves.

With a fear of failure or criticism, perfectionists avoid opportunities to take chances and do not sometimes develop their skill further. They may postpone important tasks if situations are not in their favor if the time or situation is not suitable for them. They may procrastinate until they can look good.

Some psychologists believe perfectionists are that way due to conditional parenting. The child's role in life had already been decided by the parents. Rarely satisfied parents who want their offspring to be a sporting success have no idea what they are doing to their child's self-esteem with critical comments. When they criticize, their child believes, s/he is a failure in the parent eyes. Children are easily influenced and will develop that fear of failure, affecting them unconsciously for years to come.

On the other hand, children coming from a volatile, neglected family life may think doing everything to perfection will get them reward, recognition and help them apply some control over their unstable environment.

Do you set high standards for your performance?

Do you feel frustrated if you cannot meet your goals?

Is your best never good enough for you?

Do you worry about never measuring up to your ambitions?

Do you believe dwelling on mistakes is important?

So, when you do well, do you give yourself enough credit? When you do poorly do you verbally beat yourself up? Do you punish yourself if you make a mistake. All soccer players experience failure at some stage, it's how you emotionally handle it that determines if you leave it in the past or re-create it over and over.

Perfectionism does not exist, excellence does. You are human, perfectionism damages excellence. Focus on the things you can control. Put errors behind you. Loosen the stays on your self-criticism - let it go! Don't get angry with yourself, move on. Concentrate on the next game, on what is happening right in front of you, in the present. Forget what has happened, it's history. You don't have to be perfect at every aspect of soccer and besides, team mates, family, friends might like you more if you have some frailties.

A perfect footballer is optimistic, do you think he will criticize himself...

THE INNER CRITIC

Everybody is a critic and the worst one you will ever come across is the one inside your own head. This kind of talk has a detrimental effect on your emotional state, even worse than someone in the crowd screaming at you. What does it sound like? Is it angry, sarcastic, resigned? When you make a mistake, I bet you never say "good, that's another learning experience."

People think because there is a voice inside their head, they must listen to it. You can choose.

Criticism should be constructive feedback if it's going to be of any use. If critical self-talk is not supporting you, play with the direction and tone of the voice. Like many of the methods presented in this manual, this one may seem strange at first. Go give it a shot, you have nothing to lose and everything to gain if it works for you. Is that reasonable?

Your teams behind, the clocks ticking down, you berate yourself for uncertain footwork.

Notice your critical voice and it's nasty tone.

Now notice where it is coming from. Inside or outside your head? From the front, side, back?

If your right handed, extend your left arm, if left handed, extend your right.

Stick up the thumb of the extended hand.

Wherever the critical voice came from, imagine you can move it away from your head to the shoulder of your extended arm, then to your elbow, on to your wrist, now move it all the way down to the very tip of your thumb.

Hear the voice repeat the same thing, only this time as if you hear the voice coming from the tip of your thumb.

Slow it right down, or speed it up. Change it to be like Mickey Mouse or another cartoon character. Change the tone to something comical.

Move the voice all the way down to your big toe.

You can even use another voice to make the negative one shut up.

This technique can also be used on bad memories of someone talking critically to you. You can understand this, can you not?

I'll make an interesting comment about critical self-talk. It always takes a hold in the subconscious as a command. So if you tell yourself you are going to take a bad corner kick, lose a tackle, shoot wide, then it will probably happen. This is because negative self-talk generally has a strong emotion attached to it. A positive suggestion, no matter how good the intention, is usually taken as wishful thinking so it does not contain emotional content.

If you want to change for the better, pay close attention to the words you use on yourself, they can change the way you perform. They are that magical. And when you repeat something with enough exciting emotion, you start to believe it. Use words and phrases that will motivate you and fill you with enthusiasm for the game. Every sportsperson has two competing voices going on inside their head, one is the negative critic, the other a positive coach. Who you listen to is your choice.

Let's re-program your self-image...

RE-PROGRAM YOUR SELF-IMAGE

Goethe

Using conscious logical thinking, you know the response you want to any game situation. But it's not your logical mind that manages that response, it's your subconscious which also controls heart rate, breathing, perspiration, as well as emotions such as pride, resentment, fear or desire.

To alter any poor memories or attitudes you may have about your game, first weaken them, then create better alternatives by using the methods outlined in this manual. You will be able to go into activities and situations with an abundance of enthusiasm. Just give yourself time.

Clasp your hands together in your usual way, fingers entwined and notice which thumb is on top. Let go then clasp your hands again in such a way as the opposite thumb is on top. How does that feel? Awkward? Uncomfortable? It doesn't feel natural. This shows that as you go into unfamiliar territory, the greater the the psychological discomfort. Your performance may suffer temporarily as you make needed adjustments to your game, but change does that. If you were to place your hands and thumb the 'awkward way' every time, it would eventually feel as natural as any new skill will.

You have talent. Can you adjust to a new position, squad or league? This method will show how you can perform with confidence:

Take a deep breath, sit back and relax as you exhale.

Tighten then relax all your muscle groups.

Recall the sights, sounds, feelings of playing at your very best.

In your mind's eye, imagine another you standing in front of you. This is the best you have ever been or ever will be, at the top of your game, every decision you make is the right one.

If you can't see it or imagine it, just know that it is there.

When you feel happy with the image in front of you, notice the way you stand, move, kick, pass, head and trap the ball.

Notice a confident champion before you, spreading out accurate passes every time, an unstoppable outfielder or unbeatable goalkeeper.

Now step into your image and see through those eyes, hear through those ears and feel how good it feels to be living that great image.

Keep this important feeling and make everything bigger, brighter, more powerful. Let it glow.

Do it again. Step into another more intense image of yourself. Keep doing it several times more, getting bigger and brighter and stronger each time.

Take a few minutes if you wish to imagine yourself in any situation from the past where you want a bad memory changed to a more positive outcome, or see yourself in a future situation dominating play, being rewarded, excelling. You can you know, forget about ever having had that problem.

Daydream and know it can come true.

Think of a future situation or event when having a positive feeling is desired. Taking a direct free kick for example. You have read the routine above, give that a go, or try this one:

Using this *Circle of Excellence* exercise builds a positive mood and creates a state of mind which will be useful in the future.

In front of you, create the Circle of Excellence. This represents that state you require. Imagine it has a color, maybe there is also a sound there, or a special word. This circle brings for you all the skills and positive assurances you want.

Now return to a time when you had that positive resource, or imagine you had the right attitude, dedication, grit.

Take a deep breath, exhale.

Step inside the circle.

As you enter, imagine the bright color shining down and all around you, going into every cell of your body, from the top of your head all the way down to the tips of your toes. Double the brightness. Hear the special sound or word. Imagine that feeling you have getting stronger, being absorbed by your body. Feel the strength and enthusiasm that glows from you.

Tell yourself you are more confident, more talented, more fitter.

Every breath you take you take in more of the resource, you are demolishing the opposition, everything you do is a bonus to the team. If you can see it in your mind's eye, you can achieve it.

You can do the *Circle of Excellence* just about anywhere. Rehearse it first, then going onto the pitch before a game or in training, imagine the circle before you as you cross the touch line. Do it as you take position for a set piece. How about stepping out of the shower, or getting out of your car.

Feeling good? You are learning to master your emotions...

MASTER YOUR EMOTIONS

You keep coming back for more now, don't you! Any unpleasant thought you have comes with an unpleasant feeling. If you want to win the game going on inside your head you have to deal with emotions. I'm going to guide you to be your most confident self and feel resourceful in just a moment, for any endeavor you choose.

You will come across a broad range of emotions naturally during a game, which may predict the performance you are going to have. By being aware and monitoring your emotions you can become aware of your optimal performance state.

You may be wondering, what is an emotion? An emotion is the mood you are in at any particular moment and is individual and unique to all of us. Love, hate, confidence, fear, they are all emotions and we go in and out of them all day long. All behavior is the result of an emotion.

Remember times when you were filled with confidence, determination, joy, optimism. Unfortunately, you also suffered anger, resentment and regret at some time. Emotions are your subconscious mind's way of telling you there is something going on that you should pay attention to.

Here, you will learn how to re-program yourself to experience more of the resourceful emotions you want. The pictures you make inside your imagination and the way you talk to yourself are known as *internal representations*. And that is all they are, representations, not real life, so they cannot harm you.

Changes in breathing, muscle tension, posture, even facial expression all influence your feelings and behavior.

Think of a time when you felt nervous, anxious, deflated. Notice how it affects your posture. Your shoulders slump down and your head may have dropped. I can show you a simple way to change:

Wherever you are, plant your feet firmly on the ground, hold yourself tall, pull those shoulders back, take a great big breath, let it out, look up at the ceiling or the sky and put a great big grin on your face. Smile with your whole face with feeling. Now try to remember that bad situation again. Notice your mood has probably lifted and you no longer remember it in the same unpleasant way.

Why not keep the feeling there. Stand straight, let your spine support you while you imagine a bright golden thread running up your spine and straight out to the sky. Let yourself relax, held up by this golden thread.

If your body is tense, it is producing different chemicals to when it is relaxed so you feel and think differently. Making physiological changes makes a difference to your emotional response.

And there is a lot to be said about anchoring...

ANCHORING

"Don't find fault, find a remedy."
Henry Ford

Remember how you can use *The Circle of Excellence* to bring about a resourceful state? So with anchoring. It's like having a push button to feel excellence.

If you or one of your players is feeling anxious about a forthcoming game and wants to look forward to the game optimistically, you can add resources of confidence, concentration, relaxation or excitement by applying a *resource anchor.*

The theory behind resource anchors is if you constantly link the mood or emotion you desire to be linked with a meaningful feeling, sight, sound or even taste or smell, you can reproduce that desired mood or emotion when you need it.

Let me explain. Anchors exist all around you. Have you ever come across an old photograph which created a pang of nostalgia? Heard an old song which was popular during a special time in your life? Smelt a particular aroma that brought memories rushing back? Do you frequently visit a location and always feel compelled to sit at the same place?

All these associations trigger memories that take us back to a past experience. They are called anchors as they anchor you to a certain emotional state. The clever thing is you can manipulate these anchors to bring back a whole positive experience.

Setting up an anchor only takes a few minutes. Read the routine a couple of times to get it clear in your mind. Create a physical sign which you are going to use, it can be any appropriate signal: patting down your hair, scratching an imaginary itch, clasping your hands a certain way, rubbing a wrist, making a fist, it's all up to you. Even repeating a word or phrase may do the trick.

Now, vividly remember a time when you had the positive ability, skill or emotion you desire. Add as much detail as you can. As you do, see what you saw, hear what you heard, feel how you felt then. Relive it in all it's glory. Now see, hear, feel even more fully, experience it intensely. Let it all come back to you. Let it build up so you relive it in your whole body. If you can't remember a time, imagine how you would feel if you had the confidence, success or joy.

As that memory peaks, fire the physical signal you designed. Sink into the feeling of really being there again, make it brighter, richer, turn up the volume.

Now break state by doing something like remembering a friend's birthday, saying your name backwards or remembering your telephone number, anything as a distraction so that when you repeat this technique in a moment, it's like doing it afresh.

Go back to the good memory and allow it to peak again. Repeat the process four or five times. You can bring in different, positive memories if you wish rather than staying with the same one. You choose. Remember to break state each time.

Test to see if the anchor works by breaking state and thinking of something else. Then fire the anchor to test if you can trigger the response you want. You should get back into the resourceful state. If not, apply the stimulus several times more and test again.

There is usually a couple of reasons if you are having trouble. Make sure you are actually reliving the event rather than just thinking about it. You must be able to feel the positive resource. Have one specific resource in mind to anchor rather then getting confused juggling several.

This gets better. Whenever you feel you are experiencing that resource as you go about your normal life, anchor it with the same stimulus you devised so you are topping up.

The great thing with using anchors is they work automatically. Think about a forthcoming event when you will require a particular feeling or emotion. Imagine everything going perfectly. Picture it in your mind, seeing, hearing, feeling yourself in this good state at that future event. Now fire your anchor.

By following those steps, you can create very resourceful states for yourself or your players. If working with someone, it is best for you to also be in the same resourceful state as the player desires.

If any states or emotions your player wants seem to be in conflict, say being motivated but relaxed for example, ask that person if they feel they can be in both states at the same time. If they believe they can, all well and good. If not, it's best to create two different anchors, one for motivated and another for relaxed which you apply separately.

Practice anchoring to place yourself into more resourceful states. Do it when you are in different positions or different environments. Go to different locations and practice getting yourself into positive moods. You can look back with satisfaction and see how much further you have developed.

***

You now understand how you can become anchored to certain states. Unfortunately, just as there are resourceful anchors in your life that can bring you good feelings, you may realize how you can create negative states. Playing at a venue with negative memories for you, or against a defender who has had the better of you in the past, can make you feel helpless and powerless. You may have negative anchors, but they can be disconnected by a process called *collapsing anchors*.

Unless you are a coach applying this with one of your players, it's best to have someone go through the process with you, as you will need their help to fix the anchor in place. Ensure you understand the method thoroughly and you feel comfortable with it before you work with anyone.

If working with a player, explain the process and what the player can achieve from it. Be in full agreement that the negative state is to be collapsed and decide what resourceful state is going to replace it. Make sure you are replacing a negative state with a very strong positive one.

Decide where you are going to apply the resource and remove the negative state from. To keep things simple, you would apply the resource stimulus to one side of the body, be it the right knuckles, right shoulder, right knee and remove the negative state from the left knuckles, left shoulder, or left knee.

Fully remember an unwanted state or memory. For example, lets say apprehension. Re-live being apprehensive and feel the emotion kicking in. On a scale of 0 – 10 how do you or the player feel about the situation? Anchor it somewhere on the body, for example, squeezing the left knee. You should only do this once. Break state by thinking of something else, then test if the anchor works by squeezing the left knee.

Break state by thinking of something else. This is important.

Now, access fully a positive state you or the player have experienced, lets go for capable and anchor that somewhere else, this time squeezing the right knee. Repeat the whole positive state process several times, breaking state each time, then test the anchor works by squeezing the right knee.

Fully relive, or have the player fully relive the event intensely and as the good feelings peak, the player should give you a prearranged sign – the nod of a head for example so you can then anchor the positive resource into position.

Break state again.

Now here's the good bit. Fire both anchors by squeezing both knees simultaneously and then let go of the left knee while continuing to hold onto the right knee for about five seconds longer. Watch for the players reaction. S/he should go through a series of emotions for a few seconds until that resourceful state is fixed. As long as the resourceful state's anchor is stronger than the undesired state's, the undesired anchor will collapse and the non-resourceful state will no longer affect you or the player you are working on. If you picked a strong, negative memory you may need more positive resources to make the situation more satisfying.

Test by asking on a scale of 0 – 10 how do you, or the player now feel about the issue which was a bother.

Future pace by imagining yourself or asking the player to imagine some time in the future when they would face that situation again and notice the response. If the problem has gone, continue imagining facing the old problem at a number of future events some weeks or even months ahead until both you or the player, are certain the issue has gone.

Next, we can talk about pressure...

PRESSURE

Ken Griffeyn

Pressure gets a bad name. It's the ultimate lie detector. When it's present it can be a positive force bringing out the best in you, or a negative one being an excuse to quit. Some soccer players break through, while those less committed break down. Everyone feels pressure in big games, no one is immune. It can often start long before the game begins. Soccer players under pressure become internally self-conscious rather than externally task-conscious. Worrying about a mistake will usually get one.

Recall a time when you felt pressure. Remember what you were doing, feeling, saying. Did you expect failure or feel a desire to win? Did you let all kinds of negative thoughts come into your mind?

Excessive mental pressure often produces mental blocks. Then anything recently learned in training, be it technical or tactical may become confusing or forgotten. Some situations can be embarrassing or humiliating, especially in front of team mates or supporters. The experiences lodge themselves in the mind, showing up as performance problems right away, or lying dormant for days, weeks or months before raising their ugly heads.

Demands on players and managers are higher than ever. Sponsorship, TV money, directors, fans all increase the pressure to do well. You have to become mentally tough. Look at pressure as a challenge to drive yourself that much more harder.

***

Pressure creates muscle tension, causing over-tightness generally in the neck and shoulders. The heart beat goes up, breathing quickens, skin perspires. Some players feel their stomach churn. A tense, stressed out player will kick the ball with a tense, stressed out foot!

When you are tense, you want to get any task over quickly. Mentally your mind races. The more you hurry, the worse you will probably play, making mistakes, creating even more pressure and greater muscle tension, so wasting more energy.

Consider this. Stress is internal. Stress does not exist outside of your mind. Soccer challenges do not become anxious, only players become anxious.

Interestingly, a way to relax tense muscles for some people is first tighten them further. If your shoulders feel like coiled springs, take a deep breath, slowly draw them up and squeeze them, hold for fifteen seconds, feel the sensation, then exhale and slowly release and relax completely. Notice how they feel.

Use travel time to listen to inspirational audio tapes or CD's. Hearing someone you admire or respect can have a positive impact on your mood. Upbeat music can make the miles fly by or listen to something soothing to keep you calm en-route.

Stop reading this chapter right now and do the following breathing exercise. Close your eyes and take a slow, deep breath into your abdomen counting to three as you inhale through your nose and count to five as you slowly exhale through your mouth. Do that five times. Notice, as you pay attention to your breathing and the counting, after five breaths you begin to feel more relaxed.

You can even enhance that deep breathing technique by remembering a time when you were on top of your game. As you breath in and focus on the memory, say to yourself a word or phrase that can represent the relaxed feeling. "Steady" or "easy" might do. Play around and notice what works for you.

You can do the following anytime. Think about your best long pass, best tackle, goal scored, goal line clearance, penalty save. All are past successes from using your skills and the good feelings they created. Stop any negative thinking and use your imagination to think about your strengths and resources. Make them bigger, brighter, louder. Remember good times and the things that make you smile.

Days before an important game or a trial, a little nervousness may creep in. Actually the game begins before the game begins! At home, the journey to the venue, in the changing room. How do you reduce pressure and place your mind in the here and now? Here's one method to give yourself an advantage:

When you arrive in the changing room, use each article of clothing you remove, jacket, shirt, trousers, one shoe, then the other, to let go of a concern or irrational worry.

Each article of kit you put on imagine you are putting on resources of energy, courage or resilience. By the time you have changed and you are standing in your kit, any distraction you were focused on will have dissolved. Now you are in the right time zone and in the best state of mind for what is ahead.

Let's see how you can drive away the specter of anger...

ANGER & PSYCHING

"Learn to control your emotions or they will control you."

Edgar Martinez

Soccer is an emotional and when anger raises its ugly head you must be able to deal with it. Anger is born out of frustration and expectation. It feeds on itself. When you allow anger to get the best of you, it generally brings out the worst in you. Anger blocks concentration, skill and technique. Your temper can hurt your team mates. Too many red cards and they will find it difficult to trust you and you may despise yourself for being so self-destructive.

You can allow opponents or situations to tie you in knots. Your heart beats faster, your breathing quickens. You are stood there, clenched jaw, bulging eyes and hunched up shoulders, hacked off and out of control. At the extreme, you do not notice other people, you do not notice your surroundings and you do not do anything sensible.

You control your mood and emotions. If someone makes you angry, you are giving that person power over you. They are controlling your mood and your emotions.

Anger can often be fear in disguise because anger is based on insecurity and a need to protect yourself. Non-violent fighting spirit is based on self-confidence. Have you noticed, anger only has a temporary boosting effect which produces unreliable results. Once it has been released sadness, regret, grief or remorse usually follow.

Players who cannot control their anger will never make great players. Have the maturity to master your emotions, not be a servant to them. That emotional energy allows you to raise your game. Many sportspeople can channel their anger positively in this way as it motivates them. Anger kept under control can work for you.

You cannot have a blind rage of anger if you remain calm. If you have an anger button there is something you can do about it. While you are reading, get yourself relaxed as we are going to set a calm button as a resource before another anger moment arises. For convenience, we will set the button on your waist so you could do this while you are standing when the ball goes out of play. Being inconspicuous, nobody will have a clue what you are doing, but you can set the button anywhere that is convenient for you.

Close your eyes and think of a recent game situation when you lost your cool or think about things that may trigger anger for you on a regular basis. Now, just for a moment, really get back into it, get fully immersed into that experience, see everything, hear what you heard, feel exactly the way you felt.

Now step out of the experience as if you are watching someone else and rewind the scene as if you were rewinding a video until you reach the very first moment that anger began to develop. Go back a couple more frames or a few seconds, whichever feels right for you and imagine a large red button and anchor that somewhere on your body, we'll suggest your left waist.

Open your eyes and say your name backwards or remember a friends telephone number to break state then close your eyes again.

Now take three deep breaths, exhaling out for longer than the in breath. Think of a relaxing time, a good holiday, being on the beach, a quiet walk beside a lake, or a funny moment. Something that makes you smile on the outside as well as inside. Really relax and get into the moment.

Where do you feel that feeling? Let it spread throughout your body, going to the top of your head and all the way down to the tips of your toes. See it as a color, feel it as a great feeling, or hear it as a sound.

As it begins to peak, imagine a big green button on your right waist. Press this several times and let the good feelings amplify.

Open your eyes. Say your name backwards, remember a friends telephone number. Now press your red button and immediately after, your green button and hold them both for a moment before releasing the red button while continuing to hold the green button a bit longer.

Repeat the sequence another half dozen times until triggering the green button automatically creates a calm response.

***

Psyching and gamesmanship goes with the territory. Cheating, provocation, time wasting, verbal abuse, lies, they can upset you emotionally and disrupt your concentration. Recognize them for what they are and don't allow them to get inside your head and ruin your composure. If they affect you, they are there, in your mind. Even if you pretend they do not bother you, they do.

Also be aware, there are two kinds of psyching – one the opposition does and the one you do to yourself. A way to divert anger is to divert your attention. Develop a ritual when you need to calm yourself or when you need a few moments to get yourself together.

Pick a spot or a mark on the pitch or around the ground, a corner flag for example. When the ball goes out of play, walk to the mark and touch it, or if that is not possible, stare at it a moment. This strategy can help keep your mind focused while you give yourself a pep talk.

Do not get annoyed with the referee even if he is as blind as a bat. Accept any decision and get on with the game, the referee will not change his mind. Besides, everything evens out in the end.

You only need one or two simple reminders to stay in control. Do something physical to slow events down for yourself. Rub your hands together, re-tie your boot laces, touch a goal post, nothing too complicated. These are all small psychological boosts for mental and emotional management.

At half-time, change into a fresh, dry kit, even change your boots or put on a sweat band. Do some small change to make things feel like it's a new start.

You could always do unto others what they do to you. Often they dish it out but can't take it. You are now taking the initiative. However, do you really need to lower yourself to their level? The best response is be mature and have some compassion for those who have to resort to gamesmanship to defeat you as they cannot do it through talent alone. By the way, humor can be a great weapon.

Let's calm ourselves with breathing...

BREATHING

Often overlooked, breathing is essential to life. But do you realize correct breathing is essential to good performance and correct breathing should be carried out at all times. Then your body is subconsciously maintaining the balance of oxygen and carbon dioxide. When you feel tense and apprehensive, your breathing changes to a more shallow, fast breathing which will adversely affect your physiology which can cause dizziness, poor vision, tiredness or breathlessness which will only increase further anxiety.

If you practice correct breathing it becomes second nature, so you must breath properly when you are anxious as it will help keep you grounded. There are three features to breathing, the first is how fast or slow you breath, second is location, be it clavicular, chest or abdomen and lastly, how you inhale, either through your mouth or nose.

High, or clavicular breathers fill only the upper portion of their lungs, so only a small amount of air enters. Stale air remains in the bottom portion of their lungs and impurities are not properly eliminated. These people always seem to be gulping or gasping for breath when they speak.

Most people breath into their chest area as mid- or intercostal breathers. This is still not efficient as their chest is only partially expanded.

Low or abdominal breathing is the best way as it takes in reasonable quantities of air and expels impurities from the lungs.

Where do you breath?

Lie on your back. Place one hand on your chest and the other on your abdomen. Breath out to empty your lungs, Now breath in your normal way. Do not force it as you may get light-headed in which case, give it a rest until you feel better.

As you breath, which hand rises and falls the most? If it is the one on your chest, well, you are not breathing deeply enough. You should be breathing into your abdomen.

Here's how. Imagine a position an inch or two below your naval and you are sending the breath down to it. You should feel your stomach area swell as you inhale. If it does not, place something light like a paperback book on your abdomen and as you inhale through your nose, concentrate on making the paperback rise.

When you breath into your chest, usually you are only filling your lungs about three-quarters full, the bottom quarter remains stale air. Breathing into the abdomen actually fills the bottom of your lungs with fresh, rich air which can only do you good.

Here's another trick. As you inhale into your abdomen and feel it expand, pull back your shoulders and head while you inhale some more, this will also fill the top portion of your lungs.

Oxygen is energy. It helps relax muscles and clears your mind. When you hold your breath, maybe when taking a penalty, you create pressure and a nervous feeling develops. Slow, deep breathing will make you feel relaxed, improve the quality of your blood, gives you better health so keeping your body and mind in the present.

When you look at the mechanics of breathing, you realize that breathing in or worse, holding your breath the moment you perform an exertion instead of exhaling, is completely wrong. It places your body under more strain because your energy is kept in rather than being released. By exhaling naturally, allows for more power. Kick the ball then and you feel your muscles working all the way into the follow through, enabling you to put speed or distance on the ball.

Feeling more comfortable? You are ready to experience something new about relaxation...

RELAXATION

Some people think of relaxation as sitting in front of the TV, going to the pub, spending time with family and friends. These may be relaxing times but they still require a degree of emotional, mental and physical stimulation. True relaxation is a moment of emotional, mental and physical quiet. Breathing and heart rate slows, muscles relax and you feel calm and at peace in your body.

Here I will describe progressive relaxation which is a relaxation routine where you start from the top of your head and work all the way down through your various muscle groups. Progressive relaxation was developed by Dr Edmund Jacobson sometime in the 1920s as a way a person can easily relax their whole body from the top of their head to the tip of their toes. It was an effective, but slow process which was modified by other therapists, Richard Suinn, then Herbert Benson in the 1970s as a simple way of relaxing the muscles of the body and the mind.

Relaxation itself is valuable to health as it relieves mental and physical tension. When your body and mind are at ease other mental skills become unlocked, then any progress toward mental training, self-esteem, goal-setting or concentration can be smoothly accomplished by you.

Close your eyes if you want.

Take a deep breath and clench a fist tightly and hold for three seconds, imagining the tension in the fist is a color, light or electricity, something which will represent tension for you.

Relax your fist as you exhale slowly.

Imagine the muscle tension change color, or change the substance, feel it dissolve or melt away. Notice the difference in your hand before and after it was clenched and the relaxation you should feel now.

Do the same with the other hand and in the future, you can clench both fists at the same time.

Breath in slowly, carry on with the muscles of both arms, really tense them, imagine the colors or shapes, however you imagine the tension to be, then release and exhale as the color or shape changes, let the arms relax and enjoy the feeling.

What other part of your body shall we relax next?

How about your face. Really scrunch your face up and notice how good it feels when you relax it.

Shrug your shoulders up, hold, then go through the relaxation procedure. Just let go.

Next your chest and back, start to feel like a rag doll.

Now onto your waist.

Proceed to your hips and buttocks, tense and relax them.

As you breath out, you might think about the feelings in your legs, Tense the thighs, let them go. Feel yourself sinking into the floor.

The calf muscles getting loose and limp, sinking down.

Finally your feet, all the tension draining away.

Isn't it interesting how your body relaxes without trying too hard. Enjoy the feeling of calm. You can go through this exercise as many times as you wish, just notice how relaxed you feel at the end.

***

You can do that relaxation quickly. Tense and relax your upper body as a whole, then the lower body, then the legs. Do this physical relaxation for a few seconds to stay alert and remain fresh mentally when the ball goes out of play.

You might even utilize this relaxed state by making positive suggestion to yourself.

Another way to do this is without tensing any muscles just before sleeping as you lie in bed, as physically tensing any muscles may keep you awake. Imagine a wave of relaxation soothing its way down through your body. Maybe you can imagine a soft color, one that can really relax you, going into every fiber of your body. Remember a time and place of peace, a sanctuary perhaps, gazing at the stars on a clear summer evening or lying on the beach, hearing the waves gently lap onto the shore. Engage in the moment.

***

Here are some more relaxation techniques you can have a go at:

This is an ideal way to produce instant, physical relaxation which comes from Yoga. Breath through your eyes. That's right! Imagine as you inhale, the air you are breathing is entering your body through your eyes. You can actually feel your muscles relax even if your eyes are open or shut. It happens all by itself.

Do you have a pet? Playing with an animal has proven to increase serotonin levels with a feeling of calm.

Close your eyes and remember a happy moment. If you can imagine a place in your body where that memory is stored where would it be? Now find the atom or cell in the middle of that area that holds that happy memory, imagine it smiling as it spreads itself outward toward the other atom or cells in your body.

Meditate or do self-hypnosis for twenty minutes a day, it's the equivalent to four hours of sleep.

Now you know how to relax, let's see how you rest...

OREST

"The ancestor of every action is a thought."
Ralph Waldo Emerson

When we do competitive sport, there is often damage caused to the body because the will to fight and the will to win makes the body tense, and then injuries may occur.

Your mind and body have their own way to rest and recharge their batteries. This happens about every ninety minutes when they stop external focus and spend around fifteen minutes to rest and replenish. This is known as the *ultradian rhythm*. When you find yourself daydreaming and a soft feeling of comfort begins in your body, that is it. Busy people constantly ignore these signs so place themselves into overload. If you go with it you will feel refreshed and have better concentration after.

You can deepen the experience by self-hypnosis, meditation, or by listening to relaxing music. Imagine yourself in a favorite place, an exotic beach, or an oasis of peace and calm, a garden, somewhere that is special for you. Your nervous system cannot tell the difference between a real or an imagined event so fool it into believing it's on holiday.

Do this exercise to improve well-being once or twice a day, it does not take long and is a variation on the relaxation exercise I described earlier:

Place your attention on your feet and notice any feeling in them, coldness, warmth, weight.

Take a deep breath and as you exhale, imagine a warm, pleasant feeling begin in your feet. You can imagine there is a color.

When you are ready, take another deep breath and imagine that warm, relaxed feeling traveling up to your knees. As it does, say a word like "relax" or "peace" or give each stage a number. Let that comfortable feeling penetrate your muscles and bones, soothing them.

When you are ready, take another gentle breath and imagine the feeling rising up to your waist and repeat your special word or the next number.

With the same breathing pattern, let that feeling of ease and relaxation arrive at your shoulders, soothing them as you say your special word.

Next, let that relaxation flow from your shoulders down to your arms and into your hands and fingers.

Again, breath and let the feeling flow all the way up your face to the top of your head.

Say the word or number and let the feeling spread all over your body.

In your mind say that word and imagine the relaxation double and float down from your head so it mixes with those good feelings already going on inside your body.

As this relaxation drifts down your body, imagine any tension being washed down and away out of your feet so it makes room for new, refreshing energy, spreading down from your head, until you feel your body glow with energy from your head to your feet.

Now, take a few moments to really bask in that feeling of relaxation.

If you want, do it again. The more you practice, the better it becomes.

Just allow whatever happens to happen and feel satisfied with what you are accomplishing.

Maybe you will think of soft eyes...

SOFT EYES

"The keeper was unsighted – he still didn't see it."
Ron Atkinson

You will see the benefit of this technique as it gives you additional awareness of what's going on around you. This technique has been used by experienced martial artists for many years as it helps them to remain calm and centered no matter what situation they are facing.

If you have watched any old Bruce Lee movies, you may notice in the big fight scenes he often appears to be looking at his opponents feet. Actually he is placing his attention into a neutral area so he has awareness of any movement within his *peripheral* vision.

You use focused vision when you are concentrating your gaze on a particular object so you can see all the details. Reading this book you are doing so with focused vision.

When you use focused vision it stimulates your *sympathetic nervous system* so your heart rate and blood pressure rise and your blood vessels constrict. These are all part of the stress response.

On the other hand, using peripheral vision allows you to see the bigger picture and notice what is going on around you. Peripheral vision stimulates the *parasympathetic nervous system* or the part that slows your heart rate, relaxes your muscles and increases gland and intestinal action, so doing away with all stressful elements..

You may appreciate using your peripheral vision during a match will not only keep you calm while remaining alert, but importantly, peripheral vision helps you detect any movement happening 180 degrees or thereabouts around you. If you are a defender running back toward the goal while the opposition are mounting an attack you need all round awareness to keep the back line solid.

Here's how to do it:

The first time you practice, be in a normal sized room. On the opposite wall place an object, a piece of paper perhaps, about 25 – 50 mm in diameter, roughly at head height. Be at the opposite wall, look at the wall ahead and keeping your eyes still, gaze at the object and notice how far you can see around it, to the top, bottom and both sides.

Here's the key. Place your attention on the top back part of your head, the place where someone would wear a skull cap. To help yourself, you can touch that top, back part of your head first to give yourself a sensation of where to place your attention.

Next, as you fix your eyes on the object again and keep them there, while also placing your attention on the top back part of your head. Notice your field of vision has opened up. Are you aware of the wall either side of the object, above and below it? You may see most or even all of the wall facing, to the corners, the ceiling, the floor. Even though you are looking in the direction of the object, your awareness should have opened up to everything around it. That's soft eyes!

Standing or sitting there relaxed, while thinking about that fixed point of attention at the back of your head, raise your arms out directly to your sides so they are level with your head. Without moving your eyes from the object, are you aware of your hands? Wiggle your fingers.

Notice how relaxed you may feel and your breathing is softer.

Do the exercise a couple more times so you get familiar with it and begin to recognize the feeling of attention on the top, back part of your head. At first, some people may feel a bit spacey but they get used to it.

In training practice using soft eyes as often as you are able until you begin to use it naturally. Once you get used to using soft eyes, you can lower your eyes as you would do with the ball at your feet and remain alert to what is going on around you. This is something that does need frequent practice. Give it time and build up until you feel comfortable with the technique, then you should be able to get into soft eyes instantly in a real match and it will also help you remain composed and in control of your emotions.

A further benefit to the technique is in driving your car. You will give yourself a much wider view of the road and become more aware of traffic coming up beside you.

Better answers come with creative questions...

CREATIVE QUESTIONS

Asking questions is about the easiest and powerful tool you can use to transform yourself for the better and challenge your mind.

Questions direct your focus of attention. If your crosses are poor, notice how you question your crossing ability. Simply ask yourself, "how can I ask this in a positive way?" which makes the question more empowering.

Many sports people get frustrated because they ask negative questions. "Why can't I?" To understand the question, your mind automatically looks for the reason why it cannot. But no matter what the answer is you are still accepting the fact that you cannot do it. You are also reinforcing the problem in your mind. Here's the trick.

Change *why* into *how*. Ask yourself, "how can I do this?" This assumes it can be done and there can be a number of ways it can be done so the question allows your mind to search out a positive solution.

You will be delighted to discover how you can go further. You might ask "how shall I train using the cones today?" Instead, ask "how should I train using the cones today to improve ball skills and enjoy every minute?"

Ask questions that focus on the positive:

How can my stamina problem be solved easily?

How can I stop inconsistent shooting?

How can I practice against being offside?

How can sports psychology make me a better player?

How am I going to become...?

These questions put your brain into a more resourceful state. If you're not happy with an answer, change the way you ask the question.

Here's another one for you. When you want to know the answer to something, ask the question about ten times and notice what you come up with. Your brain will keep searching until a happy solution is found. It's good to know that your subconscious has the answer to all the questions you will ever ask. You can allow new answers to come to you.

Ask yourself these:

> *Do you love soccer so much you would pay to play it?*

> *How passionate do you feel about soccer?*

> *What would you do if you had unlimited ability?*

> *Can you identify your ideal soccer role?*

> *What difference would it make if you could improve 10 – 20%?*

Curiosity creates questions. By bringing your vivid imagination into play as you ask creative questions you build up a vivid representation of the answer, then amplify it. Make it a sensory rich experience. Turn the color brighter, the sound louder, the feeling stronger. By regularly concentrating on what you want, you condition your mind to attract more of it.

If you ever find it hard to bring an answer to mind, remember the solution to it! Remembrance was a Buddhist philosophers trick. Instead of asking your mind to search for an answer to a challenge, simply ask your mind to remember it. Again the presupposition that you once knew the answer actually exists, so eliminates the anxiety of helplessness you may endure.

Many apprehensions and worries are caused by not giving your mind something better to do. Look at it this way, the one asking the questions is usually the one holding the cards.

Good answers from good questions often come to you with goals...

GOALS

"People are not lazy, they simply have impotent goals – that is, goals that do not inspire them."
Anthony Robbins

Can't get enough now can you! A goal here is a mental representation of something you wish to achieve within a given time frame. Aiming for goals is a simple way to keep yourself motivated, evaluate progress, create emotion and achieve something. A goal can give you clearer direction - if you don't know where you are going you will probably end up somewhere else. Talent will take you so far, setting goals goes with mental training and hard work.

Even with the greatest energy and enthusiasm, if you do not set specific goals, your season could be directionless and unfulfilling. It is advisable that you set specific goals at the start of the season to avoid poor motivation and any down turns in your mindset.

What would you do if you knew you could not fail? Goals can stop you stumbling through life. Why leave things to chance? Goals can help you move away from any limitations. Goals can make you the team's general.

Focus your mind on a target and you are more likely to achieve it. If you do not aim for goals your efforts will go astray. Set time limits, but keep them flexible, reaching the goal is the important element not the time frame. If you cannot reach the time frame, simply reassess the goal and keep on until it is reached.

To give yourself the best chance, you must understand how to set goals to improve any chance of success. Consider the following factors when forming goals, they help apply purpose to creating a well-formed outcome. Ensure they are stated positively and they are toward what you want, not what you do not want and that they can be well maintained.

A well known acronym for setting goals is SMART.

The S is for *Specific*. The more specific, the easier it will become to figure if you are on target. Be careful about Specific. "I want to score 20 goals a season," is specific. What happens when you have scored the 20 goals? "I want to score more than 20 goals a season " gives you room to go further.

M is *Measurable*. Create a start point from where you can measure your improvements.

A stands for *Achievable*. Only you or your coach know if the goal is achievable. Is it too challenging or not challenging enough? Is it high enough to inspire solid hope of reaching it?

R is *Realistic*. Do you have the resources and skills to carry you to your goal? Would more training be required? Do you have the confidence? If the target is too far away it can damage your motivation.

And T is *Time*. An accomplishment date. "By the end of the season," is not precise enough. What day or month do you plan to reach your goal? Make it challenging.

***

Bring in all the senses of sight, hearing, feeling, even taste and smell when you form your goal. State your goal in the present as if it is already exactly how you want it to be. Are there any negative consequences of you achieving your goal? Think about it.

What do you want to accomplish in soccer? It starts when you set goals. It is the first step into putting your dreams into action.

Ask goal oriented questions:

What do you want from soccer? Is it specific, definite, measurable?

Can you maintain the goal?

What stops you from having that goal?

What resources have you? Are they emotional, financial, mental, physical, spiritual?

On a scale of 0 – 10, what would 10 be like as the very best? And, what would 0 be like? What is the closest to 10 you have ever been? Where are you on that scale right now? What would it take to go two points higher? I bet you can do twice as good as you are doing!

***

How you design your goal makes a big difference. The bigger the better. Your goal should excite and scare you at the same time. If it frightens you a little, it shows you are facing any fear of failure but you are not backing down.

Break the ultimate goal down into smaller parts until each step is easier for you to take action. By having a number of smaller chunks to work on, stops you freaking out over a large, overwhelming one. State goals with joy and act as if they are already a reality. Read or recite those goals every day. Your mind needs constant repetition to accept your aims deeply and subconsciously. Be consistent.

When you set your sights on a goal wholeheartedly, your subconscious will do what it can to help you reach it. It does not take much to get things started, just a simple thought or action. Or even better, a thought and action combined.

It is vital you believe you will achieve the goals you have set. The happier you are about them, you speed up the results. Do you want to achieve your goal so much you can almost taste it? Keep your dream alive with laughter and fun. If it becomes an effort, momentum slows. To support yourself and maintain motivation, celebrate or give yourself a small gift when you reach 80% of your goal.

Here is one goal you should aim for. Learn and practice the Rules of the Game, especially Offside. It is important playing in any position to understand totally the rules as they will have a dramatic influence on your performance.

Goals give you growth. They can transform your life. Grab any evidence that shows you are achieving your target or that motivates you. Hold it in your hands, smell it, let it shine on you.

I cover more on goals in the *Self-Hypnosis for Soccer* section which comes later.

Let's change anything negative by re-framing...

RE-FRAMING

"Failure is an attitude, not an outcome."
Harvey Mackay

Failure is not the end result. Some people see failure as an excuse to give up, others think about failure so much it becomes the best way to repeat it. Others, you included, can see things in a positive light by re-framing any situation. The glass becomes half full, never half empty. You are in control. Re-framing gives you the flexibility to make situations work for you.

In a trial, do you think you may never reach the required level? Do you worry you will lose your next game? Thoughts like these hamper performance. If you are afraid of losing your dominant thought is about losing. Winners think about the next game and how to win it, losers think about the last one and who to blame. Notice your thoughts and change them into positives.

When you come across an opponent who is bigger, faster, or more experienced than you, don't tell yourself s/he is better than you. No! Play on any weakness they have, real or perceived. In your mind change their appearance, remember how to do that from the *Imagination* chapter? This gives your mind something better to do and gives you the confidence to face them. Being more relaxed, you can focus more easily on your strategy and stop any poor self-talk of fear or tension.

Positive thinking helps you realize there are limitations in any opponents ability as explained in the *Imagination* chapter. If your opponent is larger than you, tell yourself, "being bigger s/he will be too slow or clumsy, there is no way they are going to keep up with me, I'm more agile, slimmer, faster."

If your opponent is smaller, maybe faster than you, it's probable s/he will be physically weaker. "I'm stronger, I can easily win the ball." Look for their weakness, not strengths and create emotion when you speak to yourself. Be thrilled, believe you have the skill to defeat your opponent.

If you play with performance damaging thoughts, you can change or remove them. To make any negative emotion disappear, amend the thought. Change any color, put a frame around it, make it smaller, further away, make it darker. Move the sound, change it. When you have changed the negative emotion, repeat several times so it cannot affect you again.

Another re-frame can be done if you do not usually get pictures or sounds, but experience negative feelings. This is similar to moving the voice in *The Inner Critic* chapter:

> *Where is the feeling? Move it to your thumb, or big toe.*
>
> *Does it have a shape? Change the shape.*
>
> *What texture does it have? Change that.*
>
> *What temperature does it have? Change it to cold or warm.*
>
> *Change any element until all the negative feeling is eliminated.*

Whenever you realize you have made a negative statement, restate what you just said into a positive by beginning the sentence with "in the past." So, "I always deliver poor corners," can now become "in the past I used to deliver poor corners."

Re-framing can transform you, bring hope from hopelessness, turn despair into delight, build success from apathy. As with everything taught here, you have to practice, then practice some more, but once you have it, you have it for life.

New thinking = Better thinking = Better ability = Better you.

We often brand ourselves a failure when we forget our successes. Look at any setback as an opportunity for a comeback. Change your thinking, change your soccer. Go for change, don't be afraid.

Re-framing can also help internal conflict...

INTERNAL CONFLICT

Imagine a penalty. You are the goalkeeper. To keep the net safe do you go left, right or hope the shot comes straight at you? What if you are taking the penalty kick? Part of you may have the confidence to place the ball into the bottom left corner while another part of you may want to be cautious, preferring to blast the ball with power. A tug-of-war is going on between ambition versus anxiety. If you are indecisive in your mind, how is your body going to know what to do?

If two mind states occur at the same time, you can modify each, then reform them into a third state, which becomes an integration of the original two.

Throughout this book, you will learn methods which will get your mind working. Some may appear silly, others uncomfortable, some may completely challenge your way of thinking. Change does that. Take it as a good sign – it's not for the fainthearted.

This process can cause changes:

I'll use the above example of the two conflicting beliefs, confidence and caution. Find a quiet place where you are not going to be disturbed and get yourself relaxed. Think about the situation causing internal conflict.

Place your hands in front of yourself, palms up. Imagine the confident part of you in your dominant hand. Picture it as a color, shape, a person, anything that can make it real for you.

Do the same now with your other hand, where you place your cautious part.

Ask the confident part what its positive intention is for you. Continue asking until you get a feeling of an answer even if you think you are imagining it.

Next, ask the cautious part what its positive intention is for you.

Keep asking until you recognize on some level, that they both want the same outcome. Go through the process even if you think your imagination is playing tricks, its not.

This is for reference:

Confident part = more courage = responsibility = scoring = success.

Cautious part = anxious = safety = scoring = success.

Now imagine there is a Success Part there between your hands, possessing the resources of confidence and caution.

Slowly bring your hands together until those two separate parts become an integrated whole.

Bring your hands up to your chest and imagine you are allowing the new integrated part to step inside you.

Convinced?

***

Next is a slightly different and quicker method to change a negative response into a positive:

Bring to mind a problem or bad memory you have. What would its solution or opposite be where you want a desirable outcome?

Place your non-dominant hand about 18 inches in front of your face and project the problem onto it. Have your dominant hand behind you back.

Practice by changing hands so your dominant hand is before your face, while the other goes behind your back. Now project the solution or opposite onto your dominant hand.

Now you know the movement, get set up as before with the problem hand before your face and as fast as you can, change hands. You can even use a motivational word or use a sound as you change.

Break state by shaking off your hands, repeating your phone number, or some other distraction.

Repeat ten times. You should be able to neutralize the problem and replace it with a beneficial condition.

As you practice, it gets easier to resolve any internal conflict.

You should hold onto your seat as you are entering the world where there are no limitations. Let's talk about motivation...

MOTIVATION

*"What a great day for football, all we need is
some green grass and a ball."*

Bill Shankly

Motivation is a much used word in sport. It comes from the Latin word meaning 'to move.' The most important thing for you however, is to love your soccer.

Most people can access unhappiness, guilt, even depression quite easily. By thinking about some failure in your life you open up undesirable emotions. The opposite can be the same. You can feel confident, excited, happy, you do not have to have a reason.

When you have played well in the past, you can repeat that by accessing the same levels of arousal that you experienced at that good time.

Here are some methods to increase motivation:

Change livens things up, so you can vary your training routine, go for different exercises, a new location perhaps.

Decreasing your rate of breathing will affect your nervous system. Slow, deep breathing through your nose creates relaxation in body and mind. Re-read the *Breathing* chapter.

Someone could label their nervous energy before a game as anxiety. You could label it as excitement. Rename nervousness, boredom, drudgery into something more inspiring. How does another type of excitement sound, or adventurous.

Release any tense, nervous energy by moving the muscles before a game. Tense, then relax each muscle group. You should do something similar during a warm up anyway.

Use key words that can excite or inspire you. Easy, power, winner, even your name, team name or nickname spoken with excitement. Create words or phrases that are personal, but powerful for you.

Use up-beat music to arouse you. On the pitch, replay it in your head.

Suppose you have a boring task ahead of you. Picture something that motivates you, then trick your mind into changing that chore so it looks and feels exactly the same as the one that gets you going. As you have learned, altering the variables, brightness, color, position, shape, size, or sound can change how you react.

These are the steps:

Remember something that pleased you, a triumph you would wish to experience again. Maybe the result of your last cup game. Concentrate on that while you ask yourself:

Is it a still picture or moving?

Is it in color or black & white?

Is it close to you or further away?

What size?

Are you inside it, as if the scene is wrapped around you, or outside and you are looking in?

If any movement, is it fast or slow?

If the image is in front of you, are you looking from above, or below it?

Look at the boring task you want to feel motivated about. Ask yourself the same questions and notice what's different or the same about the two pictures?

Move the boring picture into the space occupied by the pleasant picture. Change everything to make it look and feel the same as the triumphant picture.

Intensify it, make it vibrant. Give it more of what you have given it. Hear the band playing a theme tune. Even imagine pressure on your back as if someone was pushing you into the picture. Make it real.

Do this change quickly, forcefully. Do it five times, breaking state between each change, so your starting as new each time.

By telling your brain to represent the tedious picture in this exciting new way, the happy changes you make tell your brain "I don't want this, I want this!" So, how do you feel about the boring task? It should feel better, more achievable.

***

Remember earlier, by changing 'why' into 'how' can be inspiring? Here is another word to change to get that motivation flowing. 'Should' gives people a feeling of guilt when they 'should do' but don't. Turn 'should' into 'want.' "I should practice corners," or "I should concentrate facing a free kick." How do those statements make you feel in your body? Let them become, "I want to practice corners," and "I want to concentrate facing free kicks." Is that 'want' feeling now different from the 'should?' Has it made you feel more determined? Does it give you a prideful desire to achieve? 'Want power' can be better than 'will power.'

I have mentioned before use language carefully. Words represent something, they are like symbols. Your words literary become your world. Here are some more you can play with:

Turn 'but' into 'and.' "Great dribble but get your cross over quicker." That 'but' cancels out any good comment that became before it by sounding critical. Using 'and' keeps the comment more positive.

'Try' and 'hope' are two words you must remove from your vocabulary for the confusion they create in your subconscious. When you 'hope' for something your subconscious mind automatically puts it into the unreachable section of your mind. What you 'try' and 'hope' to do will be difficult and sets you up for failure. Here's why. If I ask you to 'try' to pick up a ball lying at your feet and you do, you have failed! Why? Because I did not ask you to pick up the ball, I asked you to 'try.' Have you ever felt uncertainty when someone asked you to 'try' something? Now you know where that uncertain feeling comes from.

Read these two sentences:

"I will try to improve my free kicks."

"I will improve my free kicks."

Of those two sentences, the second resonates with the positive intention to improve and sounds more convincing. Put it like this, plants don't try to grow – they grow. Birds don't try to fly – they fly. Do you try to pay your club fees or do you pay them?

Turn 'if' into 'when.' 'Why' can become 'because.' Here are some more: 'Hopefully' or 'might' can become "I'm going to" and "I am capable." These words and phrases can be more motivating.

Complete these positive statements:

I am in the process of...

I've decided...

It excites me when...

Lets investigate the power of mirroring...

MIRRORING

*"A champion is afraid of losing,
everyone else is afraid of winning."*

Billie Jean King

Anything practiced continuously over time eventually becomes automatic behavior. Problems arise if the practice is not perfect. If it's not spot-on a player creates a varied pathway to the required standard, resulting in poor performance.

If you are new to soccer, or about to play in an unfamiliar position, you have nothing to use as a reference in reaching a particular level. Best to copy the same things as someone who excels at it.

Choose a skill you would like to master. Imagine what having that ability can do for you. If you can, remember in the past having done the skill to the level you want.

Do you have a hero? Do you admire a particular player for his free kicks, dribbling skills, long pass? Choose a role model, someone you respect and admire who easily exhibits that skill. Someone who has walked that road.

If your role model has written instructions in a book or manual, or you have them on film, get a copy to study. Do research. Find out what that person has done to achieve success. Understand how they think.

Continue until you are certain you can perform their skill automatically. Even if you feel like your making it up, your teaching your brain a new behavior so pretend until it becomes natural.

Become a film director and make a movie in your mind of your hero demonstrating that skill effortlessly. Press play and watch carefully as your hero does everything perfect from beginning to end. Watch out for any distinctions or mannerisms you need to note.

Observe how your role model carries her/himself. How do they move? Imagine how they talk to themselves positively.

This time play the movie again, including yourself beside or behind your role model imitating their actions, breathing, voice, mimic everything exactly.

Now climb into your role model's body so you disguise yourself as that person. Synchronize fully. Modify everything until the animation is exactly as you wish. See through their eyes, hear through their ears, take on the feelings of how empowered s/he is.

Feel what it is like to be your role model having that skill. Build up the feelings, sounds, sights. See all around you how others respond.

How different does your future look? How much more optimism do you have as a result of this perfect skill? Live this future, make it real for yourself.

Step out and away and imagine in front of you the 'other you' who now exhibits the skills, assurance, energy you have made your own. Make any modifications.

It is a valid thought that mirroring can oversimplify the topic of achieving success as it does not consider natural talent or social upbringing. Depending upon your physical structure, you may never have the potential to become an international center back. If you examine the world's greatest center backs, you will find patterns in their build, agility, diet, lifestyle, training and thinking. Duplicating these patterns yourself is not a guarantee you will duplicate their skill level, but it will guarantee you will become as good a center back as you can, given your genetic potential.

Pretend you are an exceptionable soccer player, act as if it were true and soon your mind will forget to pretend, you've mastered it!

Feeling good? Want to create happiness on demand? You can with the inner smile...

THE INNER SMILE

"I can let the team do the talking for me."
Bob Paisley

When you are happy, your body creates a chemical, *serotonin*, known as the happy chemical. It releases tension, controls pain, gives your immune system a boost and promotes well-being throughout your body.

Remember times when you have been happy and lighthearted? If you cannot think of a particular time how about remembering a comedy show or film, or a funny joke you have heard. Go over it again while you turn up the volume, the brightness, the color, make it all richer and remember how good you felt until you find yourself smiling with pure joy. Double that feeling. Do it again. How do you feel?

Imagine how better your life can be if you were like that all the time. Here's how:

Vividly imagine your eyes smiling, feel a glint in them dancing. Raise the corners of your mouth as if you have a special secret. You use plenty of facial muscles when you smile so give them a good workout.

Get a sense of where the happy feeling you have in your body is. Play with it some more. Increase it. Give it a happy color and roll it up to the top of your head and down to the bottom of your feet. Imagine every cell in your body glowing with delight.

You can do this anywhere. It's good to imagine all the benefits this is going to give you, can you not?

Put a smile anywhere in your body that feels uncomfortable or tense. When you think about training, forthcoming games, relationships, smile with that same energy and notice your mood begin to lift.

Here's a bonus. These happy chemicals create more connections in your brain every time you have a pleasant experience. So not only can your body experience happiness, the more often it happens, the more intelligent you become. What was a technique has now become a positive attitude.

And the more positive you can be with relationships...

RELATIONSHIPS

*"Football is an honest game. It's true to life. It's
a game about sharing. Football is a team game,
so is life."*

Bill Shankly

Your fitness and health should be good. What about good relationships? The power of relationships are the food of life so you must be aware of the various relationship benefits or problems which can directly occur in your club.

There may be some individuals who are more concerned with themselves than the team. That spoils the closeness of the squad. It could be that they have an iron-will and are determined to be the best or getting the best for their family if the club does not match their ambition. Some seniors may get bitter and jealous toward a skillful, young newcomer. Perhaps some players show a lack of commitment toward the overall team mission.

There can be hard, challenging times ahead at your club. It's best to separate them from your personal life. Any negative feelings can rub off on those around you. Is it pleasant to put loved ones through your disappointments? Best just to share good times.

Some club's team spirit has reached legendary status. Team spirit being so great it could be worth ten points over a season. In some cases, being a team player can overcome any poor technical skills in terms of what can be contributed to the overall team performance.

Are there people around who will support you? Often it's not the opposition that can be a barrier, but family, friends, work colleagues or team mates who are the problem. "You'll never be good enough," or "don't set your sights too high," might be well-meaning. However, have you noticed how expert some people can be about things they really don't have a clue about. If you take notice of people who reinforce what you cannot do, you will never accomplish anything. They place you in a negative frame of mind, give you a conflict of priorities and this all spills over into a poor sporting performance.

You get intolerant coaches who think they help by criticizing you. Some players do respond well to that approach, but not all. "You'll never make it in soccer," doesn't work for everyone. Often you go onto the pitch and make mistakes simply because a negative expectation has been set up in your mind.

Less experienced players should be coached and encouraged by the more senior team members, work directly with juniors and lead by example. The junior players then have an opportunity to learn directly from their heroes, while the senior players learn more from coaching and working with enthusiastic juniors. A coach sometimes cannot give enough feedback to all the individuals in a squad, here, the senior players can see, advise, correct and encourage.

Whether you are a professional or an amateur, if you want to live the life of an athlete, you must dedicate yourself to soccer for nine to ten months of the year. Yes, you can have a drink or two to wind down, but do it at appropriate times. Almost weekly, the sports pages print embarrassing and sometimes tragic stories of car crashes, affairs, drunken behavior, drug suspensions, gambling. Lives and careers have been ruined by some of the poor choices sports people have made.

You cannot go clubbing. You will always get caught as there is always someone able to take a photograph or video footage. There is a vast amount of coverage today devoted to soccer players and their private lives. Some reporters will write anything for the sake of a news exclusive. There is a saying in tabloid journalism, "don't let the facts get in the way of a good story!"

***

Have you had an argument with someone, maybe the team captain and hours later you are still re-living it, still seeing the person's face and hearing the words? If you change the pictures and sounds as described in the chapter on *Imagination*, you can change your feelings.

What about a conflict of ideas with a coach, official or team mate? Perhaps you should consider what they have said before dismissing it. The truth can hurt sometimes but putting yourself in others shoes makes you adaptable, so gives you further insight.

Go to a time when you had a difference of opinion with someone. Visualize that person stood before you now, notice all their details.

Now, step out of your body and let any emotion go. This will soon start to make sense.

Step into their body and notice the world from their perspective, seeing, hearing, feeling and thinking from their point-of-view.

Next, step away from their body and let their feelings go.

Think of someone you admire, a friend, hero, Saint, even a character from a book, or the past who is mature, intelligent and wise. Step into their body and see that person considering you and your foe from a neutral position.

Are there any insights you can find? What advice would this mentor give you about the situation?

Lastly, step back into your own body taking with you anything you have learned. Can you move toward a resolution? Do you see things different?

***

A key to reaching your potential is learn to listen to others. Take advantage of the experience of coaches and senior players. They have faced the challenges you now face and know how to deal with them. Lean toward them when they speak. Place your tongue onto the roof of your mouth, this quietens internal dialogue so you can pay attention to the other person. Don't interrupt or finish others sentences. People will appreciate your listening skills. If someone interrupts while you are speaking, politely ask them to wait until you have finished, then you will listen while they speak.

Most footballers don't get to play in the World Cup. Follow your goals and not the crowd. You may feel envious when your friends go to parties, often the parties aren't that much anyway. You can make up for it later. Avoid people and distractions that can turn you away from your dreams. Sometimes you may have to let go of old friendships if a fire to succeed in soccer burns in you.

One of the best ways to improve is to mix with successful, skillful people. Surround yourself with achievers who provide good teaching and will make you better. Find a few people, players, referees, sports journalists, sports teachers, anyone you can trust who understands the game. Invite them out for refreshment or a meal. Be cheeky, write to them for advice. Let them know you want to pick their brains on how you can become successful. They become aware of you and understand you are serious. Be humble. As long as you are respectful, most people will enjoy the opportunity to help you. Other people can also see situations without the emotional baggage you may carry.

Ask those involved in the game to tell you what they would tell another player how to beat you. What are your strong points and weak ones. How they see you are vulnerable.

Praise others. Being critical, judgmental or opinionated are three ways to see relationships disappear. Use integrity. Impart sound knowledge and experience to junior players, set an example by being the best possible role model. Develop their team spirit as well as guiding them to be better players.

We all get grumpy and out-of-sorts occasionally, so when you show up for training excited and pumped up and find one of your team mates in a far less happy frame of mind, find out what is wrong. "Is there anything I can do?" may be all that is needed for them to confide their trials and upsets. Most people having a tough time are not looking for a fight. When they know you are willing to be supportive, you will be appreciated.

Share your passion and love of the game. Excitement and passion are contagious. Do not allow others to put you off or pull you down. And remember, scientists proved bumblebees could not fly, but the scientists didn't tell the bumblebees!

Next, lets look at the interesting subject of time management...

TIME MANAGEMENT

"Put your hand on a hot stone for a minute, it seems like an hour. Sit with a pretty girl for an hour, it seems like a minute."
Albert Einstein

You cannot control time, it just moves on. If you are a goal down during injury time the clock appears to quickly tick away. You cannot buy time, save it, trade it or make it. Each and every moment passed is a moment gone that will never pass again. Your time therefore, is valuable to you. The good thing is time is free.

If you cannot control time, you need to know how to manage what you do with your time. Learn to manage yourself. Remember your goals. Have you thought about them today? Remain focused on your soccer goals as they will help you arrange your days. Make decisions to accomplish what is important for you.

Many of us find it difficult to live in the present. We remember our past experiences and worry about future experiences. Time passes at different rates for each of us. Your subconscious mind does not compare time passing by the same way as your conscious mind, which does so by clock, watch or other time piece.

Time varies depending on the circumstances you find yourself in. When you are nervous, in pain, sad, time slows down. The clock seems to drag. A couple of minutes can be like half-an-hour or time even seems to stand still. Long boring periods waiting for an important evening game can cause you to lose concentration and sharpness.

In contrast, when you are excited and happy, time flashes by.

Here is the ultimate time question to determine your soccer path. Are you willing to invest time in yourself in order to make a grand return later? What choices will you make? Will it be the pain of commitment or the pain of regret? It takes discipline if you desire championships, champagne and shed-loads of cash!

***

You can manipulate time if you imagine a situation and slow the process right down to practice or improve a skill. I'll show you how. Lets take bending a free kick.

Get yourself into a relaxed state. If you're better closing your eyes do so. Hold a real ball in your hands if you can. If you can't, pretend you have one. Feel its weight, its coolness. Notice any patterns. Notice any smell.

Put the ball down.

Carefully examine the correct movement for bending a free kick. Feel the whole process. Go through each step so you can physically remember the movements of run up, bringing your leg back then the position of your foot as it strikes the sweet-spot. Hear the connection. Bring in every sense as you feel more and more relaxed.

Now go over each element again in slow motion, at a snails pace so your technique is correct. Go over it several times making sure the feel of each element is just right. When you are happy, speed it all up into real time. Imagine yourself take the free kick as you would for real. Feel mighty, make everything colorful, vivid. See the defensive wall. Notice the goalkeeper surprised and despondent as the ball bends into the net at a hundred miles per hour, exactly where you wanted it.

You can do that anywhere. With every mental rehearsal, detail will increase. The practice you can make in your mind in a few minutes would require hours of practice in real time. Your subconscious cannot tell the difference between what is real and what is imagined which is why this technique is perfect if you are out injured. It can help keep you focused.

Enjoy the activity as you see yourself perform at your best. And remember to give yourself positive suggestions.

***

Here is another easy activity to help yourself place soccer as your number one daily activity. Get yourself a calendar, diary or inexpensive day planner. If it pictures soccer so much the better. Start your day by writing down the time you plan to train, play competitively, read a motivational book or magazine, or watch a match. Plan the rest of your day around that soccer event, no matter what. Make this a daily commitment. You have made soccer your top priority and arranged everything else around it rather than trying to fit soccer in.

In the next chapter you are going to learn to conquer fear...

FEAR
(FALSE EVIDENCE APPEARING REAL)

The reason for so much underachievement in sport is fear. You may have set goals, then done little or nothing to go for them. You worry or get frustrated about your performance, confusion sets in and positive thinking just does not help.

We all have a primary fight or flight response built into us for survival. This response will be explained more fully in the *Pain Control* chapter. We either fight or flee from whatever is threatening us. Freeze and faint are more extreme experiences. Today, most of our dangers are not a threat to life and limb, but a psychological threat to our ego or self-esteem.

What I am going to discuss here is not a sporting technique itself, however, some players do go through anxieties during their soccer career. One may be uneasy in elevators, another afraid of cats, dogs, or birds. Someone may not like flying and their team is off to a foreign location. Worry about your most intimidating opponent who you soon have to face makes your stomach tremble. As you can see, fear creates limitations for you and can turn into a phobia.

You were not born with a fear or phobia. Many phobias can be traced back to an unpleasant incident when you were younger. Your elder brother may have locked you in a cupboard when you were a young child. What if the dark cupboard was full of moths or even spiders? Since then, whenever you see moths or spiders or you are in an enclosed space, your subconscious relives the event.

Fear may be rated as the major reason why most soccer players do not fulfill their potential and it comes in all disguises, such as:

Fear of success

Fear of winning

Fear of failure

Fear of losing

Fear of making a mistake

Fear of injury

Fear of the unknown

Lets consider briefly those aspects of fear mentioned above. These issues do exist in people's minds and thankfully, there are methods to deal with them. Why would anyone be afraid of success or winning? Some people with a low opinion of their ability become uncomfortable with success. They are stepping away from their comfort zone. If a professional is frightened to death of public speaking, subconsciously they could sabotage their success to avoid any TV interviews. It is something not directly related to playing successful soccer, but certainly a consequence of that success.

The fear of failure, losing or making a mistake prevents people from reaching their full potential and creates a feeling of vulnerability. Those fears prevent most players from succeeding than any opponent. Fear actually creates the situations that stop players from winning. A paradox in sport is that fear of failure actually makes failure more likely. If your dominant thought is you are afraid of playing badly in a cup semi-final, guess what the outcome is likely to be? The thought of the consequences inhibits you. Fear makes you play safe. Fear makes you play small.

An injury can create a fear response because you may be scared of hurting yourself again then suffering through the agony of more recovery time. You may hesitate over going into a tackle after you damaged your knee in a previous game.

Some players might freeze in a new situation or surroundings. It is not what they are familiar with. Reaching the later stages of a cup competition when the opposition is of higher standard, when the venues get bigger or playing in a hostile, crowded stadium can create apprehensions.

Look at it this way, a fear, even a phobia, is an overcompensating protection mechanism. You did not learn it, you over-learned it and the good news is, because it was learned, it can be unlearned.

Your subconscious raises its head when you feel overwhelmed in any way. Sending out signals for you to be cautious, anxious, fearful. Now some lucky people can re-frame these feelings as excitement. But you may be nervous about a long pass, your first touch or facing a free kick.

Acknowledge your subconscious, thank it for the warning, its done its job, now let it go. You do not need its presence, now switch your focus to getting on with the job at hand and take care of what you need to concentrate on. Concentration is a good antidote for anxiety.

***

This following technique is known as *The Fast Phobia Cure* or *The Movie Theater Technique*:

Close your eyes and get yourself comfortable. Give this your full involvement. Imagine you are sat in a cinema, you can remember a real one if you want. The screen is blank. You're in charge of a remote control, imagine it there in your hand.

On a scale of 0 – 10, 0 being no problem and 10 being extremely severe, how high is the problem you are having?

In a moment you are going to play a movie of yourself and the problem you have. As it is a past event, the movie has aged so it is poor quality and the color has faded, even turned sepia. You will play your movie on a rectangle in the center of the screen, not all of the screen.

Compose a comical theme tune, something like The Muppets, Monty Python, Popeye or similar.

Before you press play, remember a time when you know you were confident, excited or successful. Feel all that good energy and let it spread all around your body. Now intensify it. Turn up the volume. Maintain that good feeling while you watch the movie. You may even use anchoring to create a resourceful state if the fear you're facing should get out of hand.

Now pay attention. Behind you is the projection booth. To get further distance from your fear, imagine yourself leaving your body sat there in the seat and floating up, back toward the projection booth. From here, through the projection room window, you can observe yourself watching the movie, watching yourself on film.

You will play the film of your bad event from beginning to end where it will freeze-frame. Go ahead and press play on the remote.

When the film reaches that last frame, press stop. Now watch yourself in the cinema seat rise up and go up there to the still picture and congratulate the younger you for being so brave for going through and surviving the nasty experience. It's as if you see yourself from the fan's perspective. Your safe. With that acknowledgment, watch yourself return to your seat.

When you are ready, run the whole film backward at top speed, hearing that comical music play. Then play the movie forwards, then backwards at fast speed several times more. How do you feel? Is there a difference to the memory? On a scale of 0 -10 how low is it now? Has the old fear response gone? If so, float back down to your seat, re-enter your body and feeling fully whole again, rise and exit the cinema.

We all get anxious at times, but people plagued by fear get anxious about being anxious. Accept fear and recognize it as your bodies way of telling you to become energized. You can face any difficulty and come out smiling.

Check your arousal level with the thermometer...

THERMOMETER

*C*lose your eyes. Can you remember a game you have played, or when you have been in training and everything was so perfect you were in the area known as 'the zone?' What feelings were going on inside your body? What were you thinking? What words would you use to describe that event? Really get back into those good feelings so you are re-living them and as you do so, imagine in front of you a large scale, something like a thermometer for example, which reads 0 – 200. Can you say what the color is and what is the shape and color of the numbers?

While you remember that time when you were playing at your optimum level, the reading on this scale will be set at 100. As you get back into that time and begin to feel good, anchor that feeling somewhere on your body, a wrist for example. You remember how to set resource anchors? If not, go back to the 'Anchoring' chapter.

This time, recall a time when your arousal or anger level was too high for optimal performance. Once you get in touch with those feelings and emotions, imagine the scale reads 130 or 140.

To reach the optimum level of 100, inhale and use the words you just used describing your feelings and thoughts as you exhale, say "relax" and watch the scale in your mind's eye come down 15 – 20 points, half-way to the 100 mark. With another deep breath or two, have the scale reach 100 while your anchor is grasped to help you feel those good feelings. This can be repeated several times to train you in reducing the excessive high arousal.

Now remember a time when you had low arousal, or poor motivation maybe. When you remember a time, imagine the scale is at 70 or 80. Again, inhale and imagine energy coming in, exhale and imagine the energy flooding around your body as you call to mind those words and notice the scale rise 10 points. Do it again and see it rise to the 100 mark. This will be helped by again firing your anchor. Repeat that several times more.

Rehearse by using your breathing, using the correct words and using the anchor which brings you to 100 on the scale. That helps you achieve regular, frequent visits to *your ideal optimum zone and it finally becomes automatic.*

Or learn spinning...

SPINNING

"Life's too short to be afraid."
Robbie Williams

This is a simple, quick-fix technique taught by Paul McKenna, who I acknowledge here for it. You may find this worthwhile. It's ideal when you find yourself in a shaky or stressful situation which needs to be addressed there and then. The concept being that bad feelings start in one place within your body and move in a prescribed direction. So when reversing the direction of your bad feeling, you can eliminate it.

Go through the following routine while thinking about your problem. Say poor ability to judge an early pass. On a scale of 0 – 10, 0 being nothing and 10 being extremely uncomfortable, where are you at the moment?

Think about what is disturbing you and get an idea of where that feeling begins. Usually, but not always, it is around the stomach/solar plexus area and moves upward toward your throat.

Imagine lifting that feeling out of your body and watching it spin before you like a wheel.

Imagine what color it is. Now change the color to your favorite.

Maybe imagine a pleasant sound or music.

With a flip, turn the wheel upside down so that it spins in the opposite direction.

When you feel calmer about the situation, return the wheel back into your body to where it started, but still spinning in the new direction.

Let it speed up, faster and faster, until the anxiety or upset begins to fade away and finally disappear. On a scale of 0 – 10, where do you find the problem now? Problems can vanish entirely.

You can also replace an undesirable state with a desirable one using swish...

SWISH

"I can change! You can change! Everybody can certainly change!"

Rocky IV

This strategy can bring freedom to self-doubt. The trick is to have your positive image on the catapult, in its high tension position, ready to fire, so that your mind accepts the image as going one way – toward you.

In front of you place a picture of an image you would like of yourself. Assertive, powerful, something that can give you goose bumps of excitement, or remember something you would wish to change, something that is realistic and attainable.

Have this image full of the skills or qualities you would like more of, a natural dribbler, a midfield master. Make the details vivid, see yourself oozing with confidence then make it larger, the colors bright, add sparkle, play a theme tune that is upbeat, adding vitality. Add approving voices of coaches and team mates. Make everything rich and intense. I really want you to live this, so include anything that improves the image.

Imagine this image you have created in a picture frame in front of you. It has thick rubber bands attached to each corner and they are fixed to a firing mechanism somewhere behind you. The picture is slowly pulled away from you, stretching off into the distance, so that it seems like a giant catapult is being aimed at you, ready to fire. Lock that exciting picture of yourself in place and be aware of the tension now on those stretched rubber bands. You hand is on the firing lever.

Bring up a second image or a memory directly in front of you of whatever it is that is giving you a lack of confidence, inertia, fear, under-performance, where you would benefit from a new self-image. Let's say 'taking your eye off the ball.' Drain away any color, turn down the focus so it is hazy, shrink the picture down, quieten any sound.

Before you fire the first, positive image, think of a motivational word. Originally it used to be 'swish' as that is how the therapist would interchange the two images, but any appropriate word for you can be more effective.

When you are ready feel yourself fire the trigger of the catapult, so that the first, exciting image shoots toward you, its acceleration crashing and tearing through that poor second image or memory, so that you end up with that first exciting picture before you, replacing the second poor one. If it is done fast enough, you may even jump when the first image accelerates toward you. Don't forget to add the inspiring word as the first image breaks through the second.

Notice any changes to how you feel.

Reset the positive image by seeing it stretch back again on the rubber bands under tension, so that you have before you the remnants of the broken second image. With that poor picture in front of you, fire the catapult again so that the positive image once again blasts through the poor one.

Do this five times. Each time that first, positive image shoots toward you, it ends up bigger and brighter, while the poor second image is gradually reduced, until the last time, when it is completely destroyed to nothing.

Another technique to reduce or eliminate problems is through tapping...

TAPPING

"Human feelings are words expressed in human flesh."

Aristotle

When you experience an emotional upset you experience an imbalance in your body and by correcting that imbalance, you can go on to heal most emotional or physical issues.

Created by Dr Roger Callahan, a psychologist trained in acupuncture, applied kinesiology and NLP, he devised Thought Field Therapy in the 1970s from insights belonging to those three fields, as a psychological version of acupuncture. Using a simple, painless procedure, you tap on acupuncture points on your body. As you tap in a prescribed sequence, you distract your mind to reduce the unpleasant experience. TFT tends to use a lot of specific points tapped in a certain sequence.

Gary Craig an engineer took TFT and distilled it into a simpler version known as Emotional Freedom Technique which is much more widely used and accessible to everybody as it uses the same points. Other therapists have further modified and refined the process of tapping, into TAT, BSFF, Emotrance and some have modified EFT further. However, they all deal with an imbalance in your meridian energy system where any negative emotions become trapped. The tapping creates vibrations in that meridian which appears to release the original energy disturbance and restores even flow somewhat like tapping on your central heating pipes to clear an air lock.

Unconvinced? Like many of the techniques in this book, they seem strange at first so are controversial, but they are based on scientific fact and have produced quick and substantial results for millions around the world.

While tapping, you must continue thinking about your issue throughout the whole sequence. This process can reduce or eliminate any strong, defeatist feelings, beliefs, bad memories or emotions as it can physical symptoms.

Close your eyes and think about your problem. Let's say you always head the ball poorly. You have painful memories of heading like you had a cocked hat on your head or even ducking a high ball coming toward you. On a scale of 0 – 10, 0 being nothing and a 10 being the worst it could ever be, where is your problem?

Keep on thinking about the heading problem, take two fingers of either hand and tap firmly 10x above the inside corner of one of your eyebrows.

Now tap on the outside corner of an eye socket 10x.

Tap under that eye 10x, still thinking about the issue.

Now tap 10x on the inside corner of your collar bone.

As you continue to think about your issue, tap under your armpit 10x.

Tap on the 'karate chop' side of your other hand 10x.

Tap on the back of your other hand between the knuckles of your ring finger and little finger.

The following eye movements are connected to various brain functions. As you keep tapping on the back of your hand while thinking about your issue, close your eyes, then open them. Look down to your right, then center, then down to your left.

Keep tapping and as you do so, rotate your eyes 360 degrees anti-clockwise, then 360 degrees clockwise.

Still thinking about the heading concern, hum the first few lines of Happy Birthday or a favorite tune. This humming allows switching between the right brain hemisphere and left brain hemisphere.

Next, count aloud from 1 – 5.

Repeat the first few lines of Happy Birthday or your favourite tune.

Still thinking on the problem, go through the tapping sequence again until you finish at the 'karate chop' point.

Where is your problem regarding heading on the scale of 0 – 10? You should have it down to a manageable level by the second go. If it has not reduced, go over the sequence again. It depends on how strong your issue was to start with, so it might need several rounds to reduce or completely eliminate it. Repeat as needed. You may get confused about what used to bother you.

Now I'll show you how the future can be your friend with time line...

TIME LINE

"If my mind can conceive it, and I can believe it, I then can achieve it."

Larry Holmes

Part of you that is curious may wonder about this experience. Think of a time ahead when you can see yourself celebrating a success, how about Player of the Season or holding aloft a trophy as captain while you celebrate with your team mates, the champagne corks popping, your supporters cheering, see and hear the fireworks. When you imagine that kind of future, your subconscious is directed toward making it happen.

Devised by Tad James, another psychological pioneer, a Time Line is explained as an imaginary line where life events happen and even where your subconscious stores memories. This line stretches off in one direction to your future and in the opposite direction for your past.

Examples of this would be when you say "I'm looking forward to the game," or "I'll put this defeat into the past."

There are two parts to this. First, how do you represent time? Think about something you do every day, if it's soccer related so much the better. As you imagine yourself doing this activity tomorrow, notice the direction you looked. Was your future in front, or was it to your left or right? Higher or lower? How far away?

Think about doing that task next week. Is the image further away, in front, behind, to the side? Higher or lower? Stay with me on this. What about a week ago in the past? Where were you doing the activity then?

Think about doing the same thing a month in the future. Is the image closer or further away? More in front or behind, more to one side or another? How about a month ago?

You can go on imagining the same activity three, six, twelve months in the future. Where is the picture?

Imagine all these pictures are dots, flags or cones joined together by a line, as if you were connecting the objects inside your mind. This is how you subconsciously see time, your Time Line.

The second part is creating your soccer future, then moving into it. Project yourself several months into your future, maybe the end of a rewarding season. See from your mind's eye out. Or maybe you have reached a goal. Everything has gone well, your game has improved, you are more confident, you are more knowledgeable. You also have achievements in your life outside soccer.

Be curious about your future. Form an image of that ideal scene of everything you wish to happen in your future. It can be real or symbolic. See yourself there, happy and successful. Make the image big, bright, bold, richly colored and anticipate how good you will feel the sparkle.

Now fill in the steps along the way to this ideal scene. Make a smaller image and place it a few weeks, or months before this final big picture. Keep doing this until you have a succession of images connecting the present to your ideal future, so that they get bigger each time, with good things happening along the way.

Look at those pictures you have created as stepping stones and imagine floating up out of your body and into each picture in turn. Spend a few moments living in each one to absorb the positive experiences and emotions happening there.

When you reach that final image, really get into the feeling of achievement as you discover yourself already there.

Finally, return to the present and look along your future Time Line. Have confidence in the knowledge that it is a map for your subconscious to bring fulfillment to the future you have created.

Next, let's talk about pain control...

PAIN CONTROL

"Listen son, you haven't broken your leg.
It's all in the mind."

Bill Shankly

No medical claims are expressed or implied here. You must only use these pain control techniques when you know the cause of any pain. Whatever the result you get, please continue to take any medication or actions prescribed by your health practitioner. Pain means there is something wrong. If there is something wrong, you must find medical assistance.

If you suffer pain or discomfort in any part of your bod, just fifteen minutes of the following exercise can make it disappear or diminish it significantly. Using the power of their mind, people who performed the exercise were able to reduce pain by up to 80%. Want it to happen, expect it to happen, allow it to happen.

A closed eye process is best, so learn the method first, or have someone read it to you. The purpose of this exercise is to look at the pain from a different perspective, so you look beyond the pain.

Get yourself relaxed, somewhere you won't be disturbed. Without being cynical, without judging if you are doing it right, dismiss your rational mind and locate specifically the condition you are suffering.

Now describe it. How big is it? How long, thick, wide? What shape is it? A cube, flat, rectangle, square, triangle? Is it jagged? Is it dull or sharp? If you don't know, guess.

Just keep focusing on the condition. Describe exactly what it feels like, pounding, pressing, pulsating, stretching, tearing?

Does it have a color to you? A smell? A weight? If your not sure, make it up.

Is there a temperature?

Now you have the location, shape and sensation of the condition. Does it move?

Answer this - are you willing to let this condition go?

If yes, I want you to go inside your body and take it out. You can read that sentence again. Just imagine you're reaching inside your body and taking the thing out.

With your eyes still closed, imagine it in your hand. See the color, the shape. Is it hard or can you mold it? Can you roll it up into a ball? Go on, play with the condition. Toss it up into the air a few times and when you are ready kick it away saying "goodbye" to it or "this no longer bothers me." To your surprise, you can get rid of it.

Now look inside. Are the symptoms still there? The same or changed? Let's focus on it a while longer.

How big is it now? What color? Shape? Reach in and take it out of your body. How does that feel?

Hold it in your hand. Can you bend it? Drop it on the floor. Does it make a sound? Does it smash into pieces? Pick it up and roll it into a ball again. Tell yourself you no longer want it and kick it away.

Is there anything of the condition still there? Know that you can do the process again. As you reduce the condition, mentally you get stronger and you can speed up recovery.

Gently get centered back into your body and when ready, open your eyes.

You can also use that exercise on emotional issues of anger, grief or fear.

***

I'd like to introduce you to *Noesitherapy* - healing by thinking – and here credit the founder, Dr Angel Escudero, a surgeon in Valencia, Spain. This has been investigated by medical experts the world over who have praised the method. Dr Escudero has lectured to the medical world and has been featured on a number of TV broadcasts around the globe.

The theory behind Noesitherapy stems from the fight or flight response. Way back in time the fight or flight response developed as a way for adrenaline to flow throughout the body. The muscles would be strengthened so one could fight more vigorously or run away more quickly. Our ancestors were constantly on full alert, especially out hunting. They would fight an opponent or an animal but there would still be fear, so their mouth would go dry, muscles would tense and they would have extra strength due to the physiology of their body. When the foe was defeated or animal killed there would be a sigh with relief.

If our ancestor encountered a big animal that wanted him for its dinner, then flight would be the action. If they managed to get away, they sighed with relief and notice, again the mouth was dry. That's the key! After stress is over, saliva returns to the dry mouth. We also sigh and muscles relax. I'll not get involved here with the other physical signs of heart beat, sweating, blood pressure, digestion, which have come from thousands of years of conditioning to us humans who now live in a different age. Just remember the saliva.

It is the apprehension, the fear, or the expectancy of feeling pain that makes pain hurt or exist at all. You finish a DIY task and go to the sink to wash your hands and see blood. You felt nothing when the cut happened as your mind was on your task. The moment you see blood the cut starts to sting and funnily enough, bleeds more.

If you are injured and told you have to live with a certain amount of pain, then being able to re-frame your mind so there is no pain, maybe just a little discomfort, makes it more bearable.

Use the 0 – 10 scale to judge how much pain you are experiencing.

As well as breathing deeply, your body is conditioned to relax with saliva. Use the idea of a lemon to get saliva working in your mouth.

Let's suppose your right ankle is injured following a tackle. Imagine you are eating a big, yellow, tangy, juicy lemon. Get the saliva onto your tongue. This part is going to sound daft, keep with it. Say to yourself, aloud if you can while the saliva is on your tongue, "my right ankle is now completely anesthetized, which you repeat three times. Why three times? The concept behind that is the first time you say it your subconscious may ignore the conscious command as it is busy with other tasks. Say a second time your subconscious realizes you are there and begins to process and the third time the subconscious knows it's true and activates in a way that is right for you. Besides, Dr Escudero does it with his patients and he then carries out amputations!

Take a nice deep, relaxing breath. Imagine your right ankle has gone cold, it's like a lump of meat from the freezer. No discomfort to concern you. In a moment you can swallow the saliva, just say a few affirmations to yourself, such as you feel no discomfort, you can turn pain off like a switch. Where is the pain now on the 0 – 10 scale?

***

There are lots of studies which have been carried out using hypnosis for pain relief and even performing operations without anesthesia. One of the easiest methods for using hypnosis in pain control is *Glove Anesthesia:*

Find a comfortable place where you will not be disturbed. Get yourself relaxed and close your eyes. Focus on your breathing, allowing it to be slow, deep and steady. Imagine relaxing all the muscles in your body one by one, beginning at the top of your head and going all the way down to the tips of your toes. Be aware of each muscle in your body melting, softening, as you feel more and more relaxed.

Imagine you are in a favorite place, somewhere peaceful and safe. Imagine you can see the sights, hear the sounds, feel the feelings you would experience there. Take your time.

Using self-talk, remind yourself you have the ability and power to be in control of any sensations in your body. Because you do! Accept you are in control of your mind and body as you focus on the unlimited power of your mind. Tell yourself you can send numbing sensations into any part of your body. Believe in yourself and the power of your mind as you encourage and empower yourself. Believe those words are being delivered into the deepest levels of your mind. Imagine they are being accepted on every level of your mind and body.

Concentrate on your dominant hand, really concentrate on it. Notice all the tiny sensations you feel there. Begin to imagine by using your concentration your hand will become free of all feeling. Maybe imagine your hand is encased in ice, really imagine that.

Continue to place your attention on your dominant hand and allow it to lose all feeling. Tell yourself your hand is becoming numb, no feeling at all. Be aware of all the unusual sensations there in your hand as it goes to sleep.

Tell yourself every breath you take causes your hand to become more numb until you cannot feel your hand at all. You just cannot feel your hand at all. No feeling. Numb.

When you are sure you have developed the correct level of numbness in your hand, you can transfer that lack of feeling to any injured part of your body. Raise your hand and place it upon the part of your body which is injured and you want to feel numb. Notice it becomes cool and numb. Maybe imagine that numbness as a cold color and it is spreading all over that area. Feel like you are releasing all those sensations of numbness into the injured area. Give yourself a time limit this will last for you. You do not want that part to be numb for a lifetime, so make sure you set yourself a time for when the anesthesia will end.

When you have transferred the calm, soothing, healing numbness, really enjoy the sensations as the area gets better, relief flowing through the area. Now say the word "anesthesia" or something similar so that each time you say the word in future occasions, your mind has the correct intention and resources to send recovery into the injured area. Believe each time you use this technique in the future, it will enhance your recovery, getting better each time.

You now know how to use pain control on your injuries and illness...

INJURIES & ILLNESS

Anything you read here is not intended to replace any medical advice you are receiving from a health practitioner. Any injury, no matter how minor, needs to be evaluated for prompt diagnosis and treatment. This can prevent minor injury evolving into a major repetitive problem.

There are preventive measures you should be aware of to avoid stiffness, sore muscles and aching joints. If you are with a professional club, you will be aware of these. Any aggressive training or repetitive overload will eventually over-stress ligaments and tendons, so making joint instability more likely along with the added risk of inflammation. Massage treatment can reverse some problems, however, also include plenty of Vitamin C, Vitamin E and Beta Carotene in your diet.

Three or four weeks into a serious injury, denial, then depression begins as there is generally a long time period before any progress seems to happen and before you begin to show recovery.

Fear creeps in, especially fear of the unknown as you don't know how long you are going to be out. How safe is your position in the team? And what makes it worse is you are expected to act manly about it. But with all that uncertainty going on in your head, your anguish is doubled. Following an injury, especially a serious one, many players often experience the fear of re-injury.

All injuries need a chance to be rested and recover because living and playing on pain-killers and anti-inflammatory tablets will eventually cause long-term damage. Players in Britain are so determined to get back to playing that they do so before making a full recovery. In most other countries the attitude of players is it's no point playing if you are not 100% fit.

Besides the correct medical treatment, you can help yourself by maintaining a positive mindset rather than walking around aimlessly staring into space. If you are suffering a long-term injury, talk things over how you feel with someone at your club.

You can become a slave to your mind and emotions. What you say to yourself can be a major key to recovery. You can literally talk yourself into health or sickness mentally, physically and emotionally - "I always get sick this time of year," can act like a self-fulfilling prophesy.

Avoid those dark moments haunting you as you question if you are ever going to recover. You can accelerate your bodies natural healing by imagining your body healing itself. Your subconscious mind runs your body from a blueprint of perfect health.

One of the most common injuries in soccer happens to the knees. Sudden deceleration, combined with a sudden change in direction applies forces to the anterior cruciate ligament. This happens much more often in females than males. The female pelvis is wider than a males so the angle of the knee is slightly more knocked-kneed, therefore creating more stress on her knees.

To slow down and change direction simultaneously, you need to strengthen your posterior muscles, the hamstrings, gluteals and gastrocnomies. Backward walking can help, backward pedaling or walking lunges.

In the past there was a lot of focus on strengthening the quadriceps to stabilize the knee joint but modern times have seen a rethink in favor of a more balanced development of both the front and back muscles of the leg.

***

If you feel pain or undue stiffness get it looked at. Let's suppose you generally take all the free kicks. You feel pain in your knee. Running is OK, it's the kicking that causes the discomfort. But it's still a case of wanting to play and not let the side down even if you have a little niggle. There you are later with a repetitive injury. All that kicking has taken its toll.

It becomes tough if you find yourself out through injury. You can do nothing during recovery or use your time wisely. Use any period of forced inactivity to study and further your knowledge. List the things you can do, perhaps studying a skill DVD or reading. Perform any exercise you can do, even if it is riding an exercise bike with your arm in a sling.

Practice muscle relaxation routines and mental training which will improve your psychological performance and make you more prepared when you resume playing.

Remain involved with your club. If able, go along to the team games and cheer on your team mates. Attend training sessions and contribute to team spirit. If possible, get yourself up to the top of the stands at games. You see things from a completely different perspective than you would normally see from playing or sat on the bench.

Run videos in your head of yourself doing well. It keeps your mind focused and positive. Your mind stores what you have experienced and what you have thought in the same way. This is perfect for mental training. You can train using imagination to sharpen good technical and tactical techniques. The advantage is you can go through several repetitions of any technique in minutes in your head without causing further injury.

No matter how confident you are, injuries do plant doubts in your mind which is why the mental side of recovery is so important. Now it's important for me to make this next distinction for you – you are not injured anymore, you are in a state of recovery!

***

How about an injured opponent? Is it real or exaggerated? Ignore anything they say. Assume it is for gamesmanship, sympathy or heroics. Give them no attention until after the match. If your opponent can stand on the field of play, they are fit enough to warrant your best efforts. If their injury is real or not, it can still have a negative influence on you.

Stress manifests itself in all kinds of disguises including illness. Vomiting before an important game to being nervous about being dropped. An upset stomach from a fear of being transferred to reading about your poor actions in the local paper. You do, of course, have a physical release by playing and training, but when you turn to management and coaching, that physical release is often no longer available.

Recover with simulation training...

SIMULATION TRAINING

Creating game situations in training which are as real as possible allows soccer players to practice their performance reactions to the various difficult match situations they would encounter. Thus being better prepared to face all competition demands. This way they are more able to confront physical, mental and technical challenges.

Simulation training helps soccer players better understand what they are capable of in real game situations and able to adapt to distractions and demands when they are introduced at the training session. Even if this is not possible in the real world, it can be practiced through vivid individual or group mental training.

Soccer is an outdoor game. The team should train outdoors in the weather conditions they would normally face. Rain, sun, humidity, cold, wind, all have an affect on performance. They must be prepared as much as possible by dressing and training for the weather conditions they will encounter in the forthcoming games. Even if it means traveling early into the same time zone and climate if about to compete abroad.

Individual players should learn to react to coming from behind, coming on as a substitute or being substituted. This includes a last minute change of tactics or anything that can distract, so the player can remain calm and focused throughout. Expect more in simulation training than would happen in a real game. A practice game against the reserves could start with the first eleven or main squad players being three goals down so they become used to fighting back. To take this further, there could be one or two more reserves on the pitch than the first eleven or squad have, so they are used to playing against more men with less room.

Longer, harder training sessions are not advised before a game as more recovery time will be required by the players. Beside longer training sessions, exercises can be developed where the players can only use their left foot, or only have two touches on the ball. Have one player compete against two during set-piece exercises.

Relax as you push through personal barriers. Your mind must be able to overcome physical discomfort. Push through personal discomfort in training, even include pain during any mental rehearsal so you can perform beyond it. When a player knows and expects to feel pain, they are more able to accept it. Success often depends on the players ability to tolerate the distress of heavy, hurting, burning muscles during extra time to win medals.

Pre plan what to do when the opposition does A, B or C. Use video of forthcoming opponents to analyze their moves and study individual star players. Some of your team can role-play future opponents during a training game, or rehearse set-piece situations to better anticipate how the opposition will function.

For real and mental rehearsal, the team can imagine they are playing in an important game. Go through the normal sequence of preparation, warm up, going through the whole event, everything as if being at a key game. Include poor referee decisions, officials arguing, flash photography, PA announcements half way through a move, or any other distraction so the players become used to them and don't lose concentration.

Poor referee decisions during training matches will better prepare players to overcome frustrations and the temper tantrums we see on the field. If the players can learn to control themselves they can remain focused to tactically deal with their opponents next move and concentrate on what they do have control over.

A young player can use this to imagine they are a higher quality player, matching their role models qualities, execute their movements and skills, integrating posture, composure, even repeating words or phrases spoken by their hero.

The advantage of simulation training is the players are exposed to expected and unexpected situations they face during a real competitive game. This training has the players do more than is usually required so they can develop the confidence to remain focused under difficult circumstances. Well thought out simulation training will prepare players providing they are not overloaded into over-training which will only burn players out, increase injury risk and take away the joy of the game. Adequate rest and recovery must also be respected to get the best from players.

Stay motivated with a soccer scrap book...

SOCCER SCRAP BOOK

Lars Eric Unestahl

Anyone wanting to invest time in soccer is advised to learn as much as they can about the game. Read books and magazines, watch DVD's. Take clippings or photocopies of pictures, diagrams and photos. Collect programs or brochures of anything that can bring soccer into your life.

Every time you look at them, it reminds you of goals you are yet to achieve, your role models, venues you would like to play, equipment you would like to own. It keeps an account of your football activities, training logs, events, symbols, anything that gives you motivation and support.

Do the same with a DVD/video scrap book. Watch the top players, study what works for them.

Use soccer book marks. Drink from a soccer mug. Dream in soccer bedding.

Keep large items around your home or room that act as powerful anchors. Look and handle them frequently. Use regular rehearsal time to smell and feel the texture of the ball. Give yourself a sensory-rich experience. Concentration and rehearsal brings in countless nerve impulses.

It may be helpful to concentrate on an object, a ball, team shirt, corner flag, even a poster on your wall. Study it while being relaxed. Use the exercise as a meditation session. When you notice your thoughts begin to wonder, return your full attention to your object. This exercise will improve your ability to focus and give you awareness of where your mind goes.

Get a picture of your hero in action, an experienced goalkeeper, a defender of high quality or a forward. Splice a photo of your head onto their body. Put it somewhere you can view it often. You may not posses all your heroes qualities, but you're empowering your mind and stretching it beyond any limitations. Read the *Mirroring* chapter again, then copy and pretend until you become your own hero. Learn from the legends.

Do you have any superstitions...

SUPERSTITIONS

"Luck is what happens when preparation meets opportunity."

Darrel Royal

The world of soccer is made up of numerous influences and variables, rules, equipment, tactics. The intricacies from Mother Nature and the ever-changing game dynamics that we cannot predict or control. These would have some believe that luck and not talent is the main ingredient for success.

Some individuals will use lucky rituals and routines no matter how bizarre to bring order and stability to their world and keep them from harm or accident in a belief that skill and physical condition are not enough to defend them from mishap.

With practical wisdom, superstition can be reassuring as it makes sense to have some order. You may already have a routine for laying out your kit, inspecting your boots or examining your fixture list. Have you ever thought about your preparations and come across something you normally do, but didn't? The result can sometimes bring negativity and self-doubt before the game begins followed by fretting, wondering and worry.

You may have a ritual such as a particular eating habit or are fussy about a favorite article of clothing you always wear? Perhaps you have a lucky talisman, a horseshoe or a four-leaf clover fixed onto your shin pads. A player often emotionally attaches success or failure to these rituals hoping they can enter the perfect zone prior to a game.

Not all superstitious behavior is healthy. It is often difficult for someone to recognize that routines that worked in the past have no longer become useful. Taking superstition to extreme can lead to rigidness and magical belief so that some players can get completely distressed if their routine is upset and lose confidence in themselves.

A player who dons and fastens each piece of clothing and equipment in exactly the same way every time, may have to undress and start again if some distraction happens to take him out of his sequence.

There is no such thing as luck in reality only the perception of it. The more dedication, preparation, research and training you do, consistently and persistently to get you to your reward, the more chance you have of creating your own luck.

The more you practice, the luckier you get. There is an aspect to every game that you cannot control so for a great performance you need that something extra. That something extra comes from the long, hard training you have done to develop your skill. Luck does not come into it.

You may know plenty of players who think once they get a bad run, it will continue or, when on a good run, they expect it to end. Once you get onto a run of success, there is no logical reason why it cannot continue. You will go into a barren patch sometime, it does not last if your thinking is right. Class is permanent, bad form is temporary.

See yourself in daydreams...

DAYDREAM

"Yes Arjan, I dream. For only those who can dream can make their dream's come true."
Bhuvan Laagan

As you enter the stadium from the players tunnel, a sea of color greets your eyes as you hear the crowd cheer. You look to one side and below the glare from the stadium floodlights you feel the very energy from your supporters as they sway and swing in jubilation. With pride, you notice every cell of your body seems to be tingling with excitement. Smelling the freshly cut grass your excitement grows as you hear the announcer's voice echo around the stadium as he begins to read out your team. You hear your name. You see your name on the waving, silken banners. Your name!

One of our luxurious pleasures is daydreaming. You see yourself as the James Bond of the soccer world. You dribble around defenders then pass them faster than a launched missile. Your tackling is more ferocious than Odd Job's. Injured and limping, your free kick wins your team the cup in the last few seconds of the game. Hear the crowd roar. You are the hero!

It does not stop as you get older. Your dreams may become more modest and limited but this time you join a failed team as a no-nonsense player-manager, introducing revolutionary techniques and tactics. You right all wrongs as you conquer the soccer world.

Would you call this wishful thinking? I would call it subconscious rehearsal. Daydreaming, visualization, imagination, call it what you will, when you engage in it you should bring in all the relevant sights, sounds, feelings, smells and if appropriate, tastes. Don't forget those good emotions. Make the dream full of life's rich juices.

Your soccer daydreams can be great fun. Just like imagination, some almost impossible feats begin with daydreaming. You are still mentally rehearsing your performance. Therefore daydream, see everything going right, traveling to the ground in the team coach, before going to sleep while at home the night before a game, or staying in a hotel, see everything going right for you during the game. You can do it anytime, anywhere.

Using any form of mental imagery provides a positive emotional training aid which can help you achieve positive results, because they communicate to your nervous system very clearly your desires to see yourself excelling. By daydreaming, you have the opportunity to get things right so reinforcing to your subconscious the habit of winning.

The final whistle is almost upon us...

FULL TIME

"I was only in the game for the love of football."
Bill Shankly

Time! Being physically fit and technically adept is only part of being prepared in soccer these days. Mental and emotional strength is also required.

I have covered mind techniques that can change your soccer, not just now, but progressively for years to come. This manual was written with soccer in mind, however, many of the methods described can cross over into other areas of your life. As you become familiar with them, your energy and motivation will improve.

We are all faced with opportunities disguised as impossible situations. Even a small change to your thinking can make a big difference. As you continue with your new way, you will begin to realize how much you have changed. Don't look at how far you have to go, rather, how far you have come. As you have learned, your conscious mind can only think of one thing at a time, why not make it something positive. You can, can you not?

If you do nothing, what will happen? If you do something, what will happen?

You are often the last person to notice any change. Keep an ear open for comments from friends or soccer colleagues. Maybe they will comment on how happy you have become lately, how your passing is improving or you are becoming a more, confident, well rounded player.

You should make this manual important enough to return to it several times to get the results you need. No single technique is a magic pill, but when you practice repeatedly it will soon become familiar.

When I was learning to drive I practiced again and again until I was confident enough to pass my test just as millions of drivers before me had done. All I needed was the confidence practice would bring. I didn't assume driving would not work on my first attempt. Please keep that in mind. If a method does not work for you on the first attempt, don't give up on it. Understand that these tried and tested methods do work. They work beautifully. You may even find one to be an exciting and rewarding activity.

Imagine staring into a mirror after a match and honestly telling the person you see looking back at you,

you did your best. Feeling the pride and joy of a perfect performance. The delight you have created for your team mates, the fans, the directors, your coach, your mind coach!

I sincerely hope you enjoy what has been presented here and I really want you to succeed because by your success, this manual will be judged. Have fun and enjoy your soccer.

Some suggestions were indirect, embedded into the text to place them into your subconscious.

The time to start using them is now...

SELF-HYPNOSIS FOR SOCCER

Disclaimer

Neither Paul M Maher nor the publisher will be held responsible for any accident or misadventure arising from the improper use of information laid out in this manual. The following is written specifically for someone to learn self-hypnosis, not as tuition to hypnotize others.

Introduction

Sport hypnosis can be a vital psychological tool to assist soccer players to get the best of themselves in training and competition and will improve their abilities, so they can achieve the wishes they long for to the exclusion of all other critical, negative or distracting influences which may otherwise create doubt in their ability.

When the player is in the relaxed, receptive state hypnosis brings, the critical faculties of the conscious mind are suspended enabling the player to become receptive to positive suggestions. They can see themselves successfully executing skills, moves, or the other experiences they train for. Even if the player is limited in physical activity because of injury, through hypnosis they can remain positive and overcome any negative mindset, maintain their sense of purpose, keep passion for soccer alive and overcome any distress.

***

The sensationalism hypnosis has attracted in books and on TV has damaged it of its scientific interest. Let's take it one easy step at a time. There are many myths about hypnosis, often undeserved, which I should clear up. It's not magical, nor does it give someone magic powers. Nor can it turn you into Superman otherwise we would all be flying and throwing vehicles around. You cannot get stuck in hypnosis, you do not put yourself under someones power who will then take control of you. You cannot become possessed. You cannot be made to do something which is against your moral code. You do not leave your body, you do not lose your mind.

Hollywood and the media thrives on drama and many stories in books and on film regarding hypnosis are the child of the writer's fertile imagination. People lose control of their mind's at the hands of the evil hypnotist to heighten tension in the story line. Those writers themselves have probably been influenced by a previous writers mistaken idea of what hypnosis is all about.

Even more misunderstandings come from stage hypnosis shows. Here, the participants are in full agreement to the suggestions they have been given. Those people on stage are volunteers who are fully prepared to go along with the entertainment. And that is all that is in this case, entertainment.

Let me reassure you, hypnosis is a natural state of mind which can be used as an efficient psychological tool for a player to reach full potential. Self-hypnosis can be a great vehicle to get you into the athletic performance zone.

Hypnosis is a reliable, therapeutic method recognized by orthodox medicine.

Those who are the easiest to hypnotize actually have the strongest, most creative minds, with the greatest ability to use their concentration, imagination and intelligence. Very few people are unable to get into a hypnotic state and there is usually a reason. Those with epilepsy can have a difficulty to focus, then there are the really mentally subnormal, beside senility and those experiencing alcohol or drug abuse.

With *clinical hypnosis*, I am not going to get you to bark like a dog! That is not going to cure your first touch or help you maintain your goal scoring record.

Surprisingly, you have been in hypnosis many, many times before, although you may not have realized it. A regular journey to work for example, when you do not remember the journey getting there. Don't worry about anything like that though, your subconscious is on constant duty 24 hours a day, making sure you are safe. As soon as conscious attention is needed, your subconscious gets you there instantly.

How about reading a book when you realize you have not noticed a single word because your mind has been someplace else, you have to re-read the whole thing again. Or you are watching a film and you don't hear someone talking to you until they start shouting to get your attention as you have been absorbed by the story on the screen.

These are all forms of hypnotic trance which happen to you every day. These examples show you are focused - however on something else.

Some clients think they failed to go into trance as nothing more than extreme relaxation took place. They knew they could move or open their eyes if they wanted to, they were just too comfortable to be bothered. That is what hypnosis can be like for some people. The best way to describe what you may experience is to remember if you can how you feel just moments before actual sleep occurs, or the moments as you wake up. Then you pass through a state very similar to hypnosis.

Here are some of the sensations you may experience, it's different for everybody:

Extremely relaxed.

Floaty.

Tingling in the hands or face.

Feeling either light or heavy.

More awareness as your senses are heightened.

Warmth or cold.

Stress free feeling.

Preparation

I am going to teach you a preparation routine which I would like you to practice. This has been adapted from the self-hypnosis script by Terence Watts of *Hypnosense* who has many more scripts. Do it with your eyes open a few times so you can read yourself through it, it's easy to remember.

Make sure you won't be disturbed for about ten minutes and visit the toilet before you begin. Sit comfortably. Some people prefer a straight-backed chair to an arm chair. Have both your feet flat on the floor so there is good circulation down to your toes and place your hands relaxed in your lap. There is a position where your head feels as if it has no weight. Find that position where your head is weightless and so exactly aligned over your body so that your breathing is at its best.

Exercise

Close your eyes and remember a feeling of ease and peace drifting down through your body, relaxing every muscle. If you find that difficult, imagine how it would feel if your muscles were fully relaxed. Slow your breathing right down so that you are breathing so gently, you wouldn't disturb a feather placed near your nose.

Don't rush it. Relaxation comes in its own time. After a while, you will feel yourself becoming calmer, quieter, your mind as still as your body. It's even fine if you notice you are more aware than ever before. Stay with it.

And open your eyes when you are ready.

How was that? You can actually go into hypnosis with that simple routine. You may have been surprised at just how easy images can form.

Visualization

You should practice and become good with visualization as it will lead you to success in your aims and goals. Some people think they cannot visualize anything as they cannot see pictures in their mind's eye. You don't have to see something exactly as if you were looking at the real thing. Try this. Remember a very short journey you did today. Something as simple as going from your front door to your living room. Imagine in your mind starting out and finishing. Whatever it was, that is visualization for you.

Effective visualization practice should use more of your senses than visual imagery. This way your other senses can be strengthened. Imagine what coffee smells like? How about freshly cut grass? Can you hear a whistle or crowd applause? What does your hair feel like? Don't touch it, imagine it.

Once you get used to it, you will soon be able to imagine every smell you can think of, any sound you have ever heard, any texture you have felt. Practice smelling things, feeling things, listening to sounds.

Exercise

This time, find somewhere comfortable to sit where you won't be disturbed for twenty minutes or so. Put to one side any problems you are having, they will still be there when you come back. In fact, after some mental work, you may be able to deal with them more efficiently.

One easy trick is to visualize a box or even a kit bag where you can place all your mental and emotional difficulties until you have time to sort them out.

Go through the preparation routine as before and when you are ready, recall some ordinary event that has happened in the last day or so. Remember your senses. How did it look? How did it sound? How did it feel? How did it smell or taste?

With practice, your memories will become more detailed. These images when used in hypnosis, provide an edge to creating maximum success, as you shall see.

Let's get into self-hypnosis.

Self-Hypnosis

You should now be comfortable with the preparation and visualization routines as I will explain to you a three-part routine for getting into the hypnotic state.

But first, how do you come out of self-hypnosis? Simply finish the session by telling yourself to do so. Tell yourself you will be wide awake and alert, feeling fine on the count of five, then count yourself up from one to five and open your eyes. Practice that a few times.

Part 1

Close your eyes. Bring to mind a special day that you have had, even a great day out, fun with friends, a walk in nature, relaxing on the beach. Notice how the memory starts, remember it and store it in your mind, you will use it later. Bring all your senses in now, remembering what you saw, what you heard, what you felt, even what you smelt and tasted if they are relevant.

Make everything real in your mind and keep focused until you can almost re-live one or more of those senses. It will often be the visual one but don't let it concern you if you don't get it exact, it takes practice. As long as you have an awareness something is there is fine enough. Allow it to happen rather than force it to happen.

Part 2

With your eyes closed, imagine you are breathing peace into every cell of your body, each and every fiber of your being. And with every exhalation, you are letting go of any tension. Let each and every muscle from your head to your toes go limp as you exhale and repeat the word "relax." After half a dozen or so breaths, let yourself imagine you are drifting further down as you become more relaxed, more than you have ever been. If you feel yourself floating up, just go with that.

Part 3

Remember in part 1 storing the memory of a perfect day? You can use that now as a trigger for getting into self-hypnosis. This is best achieved after getting some practice with the first two parts. To use this trigger is very simple. After doing the preparation routine (it gets easier and faster the more you practice) and once you are settled using Part 2, bring your happy memory to mind and let it help you drift down into trance – it's that easy!

When you are ready, count yourself out.

I or You

There are countless ways to achieve self-hypnosis, this method I have shown is just one. When you're in, read a prepared script or use a recording to give yourself your desires. It's always best to work on one thing at a time.

It's usual for people to say "I will," "I can," "I'm going to." This may be fine for you, but some people respond better by being told what to do, such as "you will," "you can," you're going to." It doesn't matter if you use, 'I' or 'you' as long as you use the form that feels right for you. If you're unsure, make a script or recording using both versions to see which one you better respond to just don't mix the two together.

Reading a script is as good as making a recording once you get yourself into hypnosis. Have you ever been so absorbed in a book you lost all sense of time? Someone spoke to you and you didn't notice? That's hypnosis. Once you're in hypnosis just tell yourself you will open your eyes and start reading following Part 3, read, then at the end of the script, close your eyes ready to count yourself up. For either script or recording, you may enjoy some quiet relaxation music playing in the background.

Now I'll show you how to use the state of hypnosis to achieve mastery.

Uses

Let us look how to use self-hypnosis to achieve your goals and desires.

Be sure you are now used to getting into and out of hypnosis. If not, your efforts will be wasted. I cannot repeat this enough, you must have a full grasp how to do it. The direct suggestions you will give yourself have to be compounded so practice until it's so ingrained, it will be an automatic response.

You will always be aware of sounds as you are not asleep. So if anything noisy outside happens you hear will not affect or disturb you, in fact, you can actually use any sound to deepen the trance. If there is heavy traffic outside, just tell yourself that all the traffic noise will help you to be more comfortable, deeper relaxed.

Caution

At the start of the session always tell yourself you will awake immediately if your full attention is needed for any emergency as a safety device. A further caution is not to drive or operate any machinery during your self-hypnosis session.

Goals

You can feel better, change habits, learn, block pain and so much more. Just decide what goal you need. For setting your goals, there are four must rules which apply to every goal:

Plausible & Realistic

Neither you nor I are magicians. If you are seventy years old you will not play in a cup final. If it is not possible without hypnosis it's not possible with. If you cannot control the pace of your passes, then hypnosis will not create instant mastery for you, only practice will do that. However, hypnosis can get you to the highest standard possible for you to produce those passes.

Suitable for Personality

For your goal to succeed, it should reflect your personality. Although hypnosis allows people to behave in a way which is different from their norm, that is only temporary, so it is no good for long-term goals. Select a goal which would not surprise a family member that you were doing it, then use hypnosis to speed up the process and become proficient at it.

Make it Clear

You need to know what it is that you want. Many people say "I want to be a winner." A winner at what? Your subconscious has the mind of a seven year old, it only works with uncomplicated, simple statements, not ambiguous ones. "I want to score at least five hat-tricks every season," is a clear goal. That is achievable.

Make it Positive

Think of what you want, not what you don't want. What you can do, not what you can't do. What you like, not what you don't like. "I don't overlap enough," is not a positive statement. "I wish to overlap more and competently," is. By implication, consciously they mean the same, but the literal understanding subconscious does not understand implications. "I am determined not to miss an open goal," is a negative statement. "I am determined to score into an open goal if the opportunity arrives," carries a different message to your subconscious which can only function on what is, not understanding what is not.

The Four Senses Test

You should apply at least four of your senses to your visualization of any goal. You should SEE yourself doing it successfully, receiving a reward perhaps; HEAR something associated with it, applause maybe; FEEL something associated, how about the cool metal of that trophy in your hands and then SMELL or TASTE something there, celebratory Champagne for example.

Now turn all of that into a living video, make it a rich, sense filled experience you can go over and over in your mind. As you practice using your senses, you will expand your conscious awareness.

It's best to work on one goal at a time, each goal can run into the next as you progress. Working on one goal at a time makes it more likely for you to achieve it and is a lot easier than trying to remember a jumble of scenarios.

Get yourself into hypnosis and be patient, you cannot hurry it. Once there, play your sensory rich video in your mind three, four, five times and let yourself feel the excitement of this adventure each time. That's an emotional reward for yourself and is an important part of the success plan so make it your reality.

Each time you do self-hypnosis, you will do it better than the time before. Want it to happen, let it happen.

You now have the mind skills to improve your soccer. Did you enjoy that?

Enjoy your soccer.

If you enjoyed reading Soccer Mind please write a review on Amazon. Say what you liked about it, if it helped you in any way and anything else you would have liked to have read. Thanks.

BIBLIOGRAPHY

Bolstad, Dr Richard., *Resolve.* Crown House Publishing, 2002.

Callahan, Dr Roger., *Tapping The Healer Within.* McGraw-Hill Contemporary, 2002.

Court, Martyn., *The Winning Mindset.* Trafford Publishing, 2005.

Eason, Adam., *The Secrets of Self-Hypnosis.* Network 3000 Publishing, 2005.

Edgette, John H & Rowan, Tim., *Winning The Mind Game.* Crown House Publishing, 2003.

Hodgson, David., *The Buzz.* Crown House Publishing, 2006.

Lazarus, Jeremy., *Ahead Of The Game.* Ecademy Press, 2006.

Liggett, Donald R., *Sport Hypnosis.* Human Kinetics, 2000.

Mack, Garry with David Casstevens., *Mind Gym.* McGraw-Hill Professional, 2002.

McKenna, Paul., *Change Your Life In Seven Days.* Bantam Press, 2004.

Mycoe, Stephen., *Unlimited Sports Success.* iUniversal.com, 2001.

Orlick, Terry., *In Pursuit Of Excellence.* Human Kinetics, 2000.

Oswald, Yvonne., *Every Word Has Power.* Atria Books, 2008.

Robbins, Anthony., *Awaken The Giant Within.* Pocket Books, 2001.

Robbins Blair, Forbes., *Instant Self-Hypnosis.* Sourcebooks Inc., 2003.

Royle, Dr Jonathan., *Confessions Of A Hypnotist.* Exposure Publishing, 2006.

Waterfield, Robin., *Hidden Depths.* Pan Books, 2004.

ABOUT THE AUTHOR

Paul M Maher PhD

Paul has had a lifetime of experience in the Health & Fitness industry; beginning as a trainer, then gym manager and sports therapist which ultimately led him into sports psychology. His enthusiasm and success made it a natural progression to create a series of sports psychology books to guide athletes in mind control to improve their performance. The techniques in these sports psychology books are designed to give the athletes the tools to help themselves.

Look out for more books in the The Mental Game series.

The Mental Game is a series of books written for athletes who wish to tap into the power within their mind and gain an edge on the competition. The books include techniques to improve performance, assert focus and control when under pressure and gain a precious edge on the competition.

The author, Dr Paul Maher, began work in the health and fitness industry during the 1980s as a trainer, then gym manager before becoming a sports therapist. Following fifteen years as a clinical hypnotherapist, he studied for his PhD in Sports Psychology and began writing on the subject in 2011.

Today, performance enhancement needs psychology, whatever your sport. These books teach methods which can lead to significant improvements. Practical, do-it-yourself, user-friendly instructions are clearly explained step-by-step. Just read through to understand your mind, set goals, control anger, gain belief, master emotions and gain that precious advantage.

These books are a toolbox for winning The Mental Game. When you need to tackle a problem, you can quickly find the appropriate strategy; read as much as you need or use it as a refresher. Not only will these books help you directly improve at your sport, but they are also packed with fascinating knowledge and skills you can apply in your whole life.

To win the game, first you must win The Mental Game

Have you got a book in you? Want to get published?

DreamEngine provides extraordinary support for aspiring authors who want education, expert marketing, and an author mythology that actually sells books. Talk to us today!

publishing@dreamengine.co.uk
dreamengine.co.uk

Also, by DreamEngine

Ocean Boulevard
by David Baboulene

Book 1: An epic and exhilarating journey all the way... from a boy to a man.

"I laughed so hard, stuff came out of my nose." Pete McCarthy.

Jumping Ships
by David Baboulene

Book 2: The global misadventures of a cargo ship apprentice.

"Interesting, raucous and very, very funny to the point that will make your eyes water." TalkSport

Fires of Brigantia
by Tina Zee

The Roman army. One Yorkshire woman.

They never stood a chance.

Paul M Maher PhD

Lara's Secret

Book 1 in The Pete West Mystery Series
by Ray C Doyle

It's not a good story until somebody dies.

The Blind Pigeon

Book 2 in The Pete West Mystery Series
by Ray C Doyle

It's a good story. Somebody died.

Surface
by Violet Neill

Book 1 of the Hollow Trilogy

Lucas Spencer loves his wife Adele.

She is beautiful, intelligent ... And dead.

Life's a Peach
by Steve Askham

Extraordinary fruity business you didn't know that you
NEED to know...

Soccer Mind

The secret life of an international fruit trader.

The Magical World of Lilly Lemoncello
by Carolyn Goodyear

Fate decides Lilly's start in life.
So she chooses to let Fate decide the rest of it too.

A heart-warming and remarkable work of human goodness.

<u>The Shock Tube</u>
by Paul Curtis

Anybody reading this book will learn something uncomfortable.
About themselves...

Nonfiction:

The Story Series
by David Baboulene

Learn how stories work.

HelpLoveSupport Imprint

Paul M Maher PhD

Conscious Autism Parenting
By Rachna Malkani

Eight Habits for Looking After Yourself and Making Sure your Autistic Child is the Most Wonderful Gift in Your Life.

The Mental Game Series

Body Building Mind
by Paul M Maher PhD

Think and Grow Muscle with Mental Training

Cricket Mind
by Paul M Maher PhD

Raise Your Cricket with Mental Training

Soccer Mind
by Paul M Maher PhD

Raise Your Game with Mental Training

Tennis Mind
by Paul M Maher PhD

Raise Your Tennis with Mental Training